ADVANCE PRAISE

"Patrick Cheng's *Radical Love* is an excellent introduction to queer theology. It is readable and nuanced, a marvelous teaching resource."

> - Carter Heyward, author of *Keep Your Courage: A Radical Christian Feminist Speaks* and Professor Emertia of Theology, Episcopal Divinity School

"Thoroughly Christian and thoroughly Queer, Cheng helps readers welcome a theology that leaves no one behind."

> - Chris Glaser, author of *As My Own Soul: The Blessing of Same-Gender Marriage* and *Coming Out as Sacrament*

"Patrick Cheng's *Radical Love* is not only an excellent introduction to LGBT theology but an important contribution to the discipline of theology and the life of the church. It is a must read for anyone who cares about the health of the church and theology today."

> - James H. Cone, Charles Augustus Briggs Distinguished Professor of Systematic Theology, Union Theological Seminary, New York, NY

"This book is a clear, accessible and exciting analysis of Queer Theology. Cheng perfectly captures both the challenge and the rootedness of Queer Theology."

> - Professor Elizabeth Stuart, Pro Vice-Chancellor, University of Winchester, UK

"I would characterize Cheng's notion of 'radical love' as 'wild grace' with which mainstream theology has yet to wrestle. This is a good text for introducing queer theology to undergraduate and graduate students."

> - Rev. Dr. Bob Shore-Goss, Senior Pastor/Theologian, Metropolitan Community Church in the Valley, North Hollywood, CA

"*Radical Love* – a love so extreme that it dissolves our existing boundaries! What concept could be more liberating for a culture like ours, where lives are crucified on rigid binaries like male, vs. female, us vs. them, straight vs. queer? *Radical Love* is an excellent introduction for beginners and an excellent synthesis for more advanced readers."

> - Virginia Ramey Mollenkott, author of *Sensuous Spirituality* and *Omnigender*, among many other books.

For Michael

καὶ ἐὰν ἔχω προφητείαν
καὶ εἰδῶ τὰ μυστήρια πάντα
καὶ πᾶσαν τὴν γνῶσιν
καὶ ἐὰν ἔχω πᾶσαν τὴν πίστιν
ὥστε ὄρη μεθιστάναι,
ἀγάπην δὲ μὴ ἔχω,
οὐθέν εἰμι.

And if I have prophetic powers,
and understand all mysteries
and all knowledge,
and if I have all faith,
so as to remove mountains,
but do not have love,
I am nothing.

1 Cor. 13:2

An
Introduction
to
QUEER
Theology

RADICAL
LOVE

PATRICK S. CHENG

Seabury Books

NEW YORK

Copyright © 2011 by Patrick S. Cheng

Unless otherwise noted, the Scripture quotations contained herein are from the New Revised Standard Version Bible, copyright © 1989 by the Division of Christian Education of the National Council of Churches of Christ in the U.S.A. Used by permission. All rights reserved.

Cover design by Laurie Klein Westhafer
Typeset by Denise Hoff

Library of Congress Cataloging-in-Publication Data

Cheng, Patrick S.
  Radical love : an introduction to queer theology / by Patrick S. Cheng.
    p. cm.
  Includes bibliographical references and index.
  ISBN 978-1-59627-132-6 (pbk.) -- ISBN 978-1-59627-136-4 (ebook) 1. Queer theology. I. Title.
  BT83.65.C44 2011
  230.086'64--dc22
                        2010046872

Seabury Books
445 Fifth Avenue
New York, New York 10016

www.churchpublishing.org

An imprint of Church Publishing Incorporated

Contents

Acknowledgments

This book could not have been written without the help and encouragement of many people. I would like to thank my doctoral adviser and mentor, James H. Cone, who believed in me and helped me find my theological voice. I would also like to thank my other theological mentors over the last decade: Kwok Pui-lan, Mark D. Jordan, and Christopher L. Morse.

I would like to thank all members of the Episcopal Divinity School community for their support, especially my faculty colleagues. It is difficult to imagine a more talented and passionate group of scholars-pastors-activists than Angela Bauer-Levesque, Clarence Butler, Christopher Duraisingh, Bill Kondrath, Kwok Pui-lan, Julie Lytle, Joan Martin, Katherine Hancock Ragsdale, Ed Rodman, Susie Snyder, Fredrica Harris Thompsett, Larry Wills, and Gale Yee. I am also grateful for Aura Fluett, our wonderful reference librarian.

I am grateful for my past and—in some instances—present colleagues and friends at Union Theological Seminary in New York City, the Church Pension Group, the Metropolitan Community Churches, the American Academy of Religion (in particular, the Asian North American Religions, Cultures, and Society Group and the Gay Men and Religion Group), Christ Church Cambridge, the Gay Asian and Pacific Islander Men of New York (GAPIMNY), Queer Asian Spirit, and Easton Mountain Retreat Center, many of whom are cited in this book.

I am grateful for the participants in the 2010 Emory University Summer Seminar on Religion and Sexuality, the participants in the 2010 Human Rights Campaign Summer Institute, and my colleagues in the Emerging Queer API Religion Scholars (EQARS) group.

I am grateful for my theological "family" and other conversation partners, colleagues, and friends over the years, including Byron Au Yong, Roy Birchard, Pat Bumgardner, Mike Campos, Faith Cantor, George Chien, Arnie Chin, Susie Chin, Conrad Chu, Hugo Córdova Quero, Ned Coughlin, Thomas Eoyang, Diane Fisher, Vicky Furio, K. David Harrison, Sharon Hwang Colligan, Barton T. Jones, Michael Kelly, Jonipher Kwong, Wendell Laurent, Debbie Lee, Elizabeth Leung, Benny Liew, Leng Lim, Sister Linda Julian, Mary McKinney, Jay Michaelson, Kyle Miura, Tim Nevits, Hung Nguyen, Su Pak, Christine Pao, Pauline Park, Sung Park, Ed Paul, Paul Raushenbush, Joe Robinson, Michael Shernoff, David Siegenthaler, Miak Siew, Scot Simon, John Stasio, Pressley Sutherland, Dave Swinarski, Jonathan Tan, Josh Thomas, Weiben Wang, and Lai Shan Yip. There are many, many others—the names of whom would fill many books in the world—and I am thankful for all of them.

I have appreciated the thoughtful comments of my editor at Seabury Books, Davis Perkins, and those of my friends and colleagues Rich McCarty, Catherine Owens, Bob Shore-Goss, Sue Spilecki, and Linn Tonstad who graciously agreed to review the manuscript. Of course, all errors and omissions in the manuscript remain my sole responsibility.

I am grateful to my network of family and friends in both cyberspace (for example, on Facebook) and the real world, including my mom, Deanna Cheng; my brother, Andrew Cheng; and his family, Abi Karlin-Resnick, Jordan Cheng, and Noah Cheng. I give thanks for the life of my late father, Richard H.Y. Cheng. Most of all, I am grateful to my husband, Michael Boothroyd, who has been radical love incarnate for me over the last two decades, and our dog, Chartres, who has brought much joy into our lives.

December 1, 2010
World AIDS Day
Cambridge, Massachusetts

Introduction

When I met and fell in love with my husband, Michael, almost two decades ago, something radical happened. I experienced the boundaries between myself and the outside world dissolving in a way that I had never experienced before. The boundaries that had separated me from other people in the past—intellectually, emotionally, and physically—became fluid. Michael and I were no longer two separate and distinct persons, but rather two connected human beings with permeable borders.

Other boundaries within me dissolved as well. For example, the boundaries that had previously kept the categories of male and female separate and distinct also became fluid. As a gay man in a same-sex relationship, my standard definitions of who a "man" was allowed to fall in love with (that is, traditionally only with a "woman" and not with another "man") no longer held true.

But most importantly, the boundaries between God and me began to dissolve. My early childhood love for God, which had evaporated in the face of the hatred and intolerance of anti-gay Christians after I realized that I was gay and started to come out of the closet, was rekindled as I understood what it meant to experience embodied love. Indeed, we know that God is love[1]—a love so extreme that it is described in superlative terms such as *ploutos* (extreme wealth)[2] and *huperperisseuō* (superabundance).[3] Not surprisingly, those who love one another deeply have passed through the boundaries between death and life.[4]

---

[1] 1 John 4:8.
[2] Eph. 1:18.
[3] Rom. 5:20.
[4] 1 John 3:14 ("We know that we have passed from death to life because we love one another.").

Radical love, I contend, is a *love so extreme that it dissolves our existing boundaries*, whether they are boundaries that separate us from other people, that separate us from preconceived notions of sexuality and gender identity, or that separate us from God. It is the thesis of this book that the connections between Christian theology and queer theory are actually much closer than one would think. That is, radical love lies at the heart of *both* Christian theology *and* queer theory.

Radical love is at the heart of Christian theology because we Christians believe in a God who, through the incarnation, life, death, resurrection, and ascension of Jesus Christ, has dissolved the boundaries between death and life, time and eternity, and the human and the divine. Similarly, radical love is also at the heart of queer theory because it challenges our existing boundaries with respect to sexuality and gender identity (for example, "gay" vs. "straight," or "male" vs. "female") as social constructions and *not* essentialist, or fixed, concepts.

It should be noted that radical love is not about abolishing all rules or justifying an antinomian existence, sexual or otherwise. Radical love is ultimately about *love*, which, as St. Paul teaches us, is patient and kind, and not envious, boastful, arrogant, or rude.[5] As such, radical love is premised upon safe, sane, and consensual behavior. Thus, nonconsensual behavior—such as rape or sexual exploitation—is by definition excluded from radical love.

Thus, queer theology—that is, the place where Christian theology and queer theory meet—is all about radical love. Some skeptics may paraphrase the second-century theologian Tertullian by asking: What does queerness have to do with theology? (Tertullian, of course, famously resisted the merging of secular philosophy with the gospel message by asking what Athens had to do with Jerusalem.) The answer: Everything! I believe that, at its heart, Christian theology is a fundamentally queer enterprise, and this book is an attempt to demonstrate this truth.

Queer theology has enjoyed a remarkable surge in popularity. There have been a number of significant works published

---

[5] 1 Cor. 13:4–5.

recently that relate in whole or in part to queer theology. These books include *Dancing Theology in Fetish Boots: Essays in Honour of Marcella Althaus-Reid*; *The Embrace of Eros: Bodies, Desires, and Sexuality in Christianity*; *Seducing Augustine: Bodies, Desires, Confessions*; *Sexuality and the Sacred: Sources for Theological Reflection* (2nd edition); and *Trans/formations*.[6]

However, to date there have not been many easily accessible introductions or surveys of the field for individuals who are not familiar with queer theory, on the one hand, or the traditional doctrines of Christian theology, on the other.[7] This book seeks to fill that gap in the discourse. It also provides study questions and suggested resources for further study at the end of each main section, which makes it ideal for self-study, for religious studies, theology, and queer studies classes, or for adult educa-tion in parishes and congregations.

Chapter one is an introduction to the word "queer" in the context of radical love. It explores why this book is about "queer" theology, as opposed to "gay and lesbian" theology. It explains three different uses of the word "queer," and it also provides a brief introduction to the academic discipline of queer theory and its relationship to queer theology. The chapter also intro-duces the four sources of queer theology: scripture, tradition, reason, and experience.

Chapter two is a brief overview of the genealogy of queer theology over the last half century. This chapter sets out four nonmutually exclusive strands in the historical development of queer theology since the 1950s: apologetic, liberation, rela-tional, and queer. It closes with some reflections on the future of queer theology, particularly with respect to postcolonial and jurisprudential concepts such as hybridity and intersectionality.

---

[6] See Lisa Isherwood and Mark D. Jordan, eds., *Dancing Theology in Fetish Boots: Essays in Honour of Marcella Althaus-Reid* (London: SCM Press, 2010); Margaret D. Kamitsuka, ed., *The Embrace of Eros: Bodies, Desires, and Sexuality in Christianity* (Minneapolis, MN: Fortress Press, 2010); Virginia Burrus, Mark D. Jordan, and Karmen MacKendrick, *Seducing Augustine: Bodies, Desires, Confessions* (New York: Fordham University Press, 2010); Marvin M. Ellison and Kelly Brown Douglas, eds., *Sexuality and the Sacred: Sources for Theological Reflection*, 2nd ed. (Louisville, KY: Westminster John Knox Press, 2010); and Marcella Althaus-Reid and Lisa Isherwood, eds., *Trans/formations* (London: SCM Press, 2009).

[7] Elizabeth Stuart, along with others, wrote a helpful guide to Christianity for lesbian, gay, bisexual, and transgender people in 1997—see Elizabeth Stuart, Andy Braunston, Malcolm Edwards, John McMahon, and Tim Morrison, *Religion Is a Queer Thing: A Guide to the Christian Faith for Lesbian, Gay, Bisexual and Transgendered People* (Cleveland, OH: Pilgrim Press, 1997)—but it is now out of print. Stuart also published a chronological review of developments in LGBT theology in 2003—see Elizabeth Stuart, *Gay and Lesbian Theologies: Repetitions with Critical Difference* (Aldershot, UK: Ashgate, 2003)—but it is organized historically as opposed to by doctrinal topic.

Chapters three through five consist of an overview of queer theology using the general framework of the Apostles' Creed and the Nicene Creed. These creeds are divided into three main sections, each of which covers one of the three persons of the Trinity—God, Jesus Christ, and Holy Spirit—and these chapters are organized in the same way.

Thus, chapter three is about the doctrine of God, or *the sending forth of radical love*. The subsections in this chapter consist of the doctrines of revelation (as God's coming out as radical love), God (as radical love itself), Trinity (as an internal community of radical love), and creation (as God's outpouring of radical love).

Chapter four is about the doctrine of Jesus Christ, or *the recovery of radical love*. The subsections in this chapter consist of the doctrines of sin (as the rejection of radical love), Jesus Christ (as the embodiment of radical love), Mary (as the bearer of radical love), and atonement (as the ending of scapegoating through radical love).

Chapter five is about the doctrine of the Holy Spirit, or *the return to radical love*. The subsections in this chapter consist of the doctrines of Holy Spirit (as pointing us toward radical love), church (as an external community of radical love), saints (as the breaking through of radical love), sacraments (as a foretaste of radical love), and last things (as the horizon of radical love).

Finally, one caveat is worth stating expressly in this introduction. This book is about Christian theology, and, as such, it is self-consciously written by a Christian theologian from "inside" the Christian tradition. This book is not meant to disrespect, discourage, or denigrate other faith traditions or beliefs.[8]

---

[8] There are a growing number of works about queer religious issues, including the transgender religious experience, that are written from the perspective of other faith traditions such as Judaism. See, e.g., Rebecca Alpert, *Like Bread on the Seder Plate: Jewish Lesbians and the Transformation of Tradition* (New York: Columbia University Press, 1997); Christie Balka and Andy Rose, eds., *Twice Blessed: On Being Lesbian or Gay and Jewish* (Boston, MA: Beacon Press, 1989); Gregg Drinkwater, Joshua Lesser, and David Shneer, *Torah Queeries: Weekly Commentaries on the Hebrew Bible* (New York: New York University Press, 2009); Noach Dzmura, ed., *Balancing on the Mechitza: Transgender in Jewish Community* (Berkeley, CA: North Atlantic Books, 2010); Steven Greenberg, *Wrestling with God and Men: Homosexuality in the Jewish Tradition* (Madison: University of Wisconsin Press, 2004). For helpful overviews of LGBT issues and world religions, see Christian de la Huerta, *Coming Out Spiritually: The Next Step* (New York: Jeremy T. Tarcher/Putnam, 1999), 170–208; Jeffrey S. Siker, ed., *Homosexuality and Religion: An Encyclopedia* (Westport, CT: Greenwood Press, 2007); Arlene Swidler, ed., *Homosexuality and World Religions* (Valley Forge, PA: Trinity Press International, 1993); Melissa M. Wilcox, "Innovation in Exile: Religion and Spirituality in Lesbian, Gay, Bisexual, and Transgender Communities," in *Sexuality and the World's Religions*, ed. David W. Machacek and Melissa M. Wilcox (Santa Barbara, CA: ABC-CLIO, 2003), 323–57.

However, the expressly "Christian" nature of this book does serve a number of purposes. Not only is this book a response to those antigay Christians who insist that queerness has nothing to do with Christian theology, but, more importantly, it is written for other lesbian, gay, bisexual, transgender, intersex, questioning, and allied ("LGBT" or "queer") Christians who have wrestled deeply with reconciling their queerness with their faith.

As a gay theologian, seminary professor, and ordained minister, I have been continuously amazed at the ways in which the radical love of the queer community has helped us to overcome the seemingly insurmountable religious, legal, political, societal, cultural, and other obstacles that prevent us from fully loving one another and being who God has created us to be. As Paul states beautifully in the eighth chapter of his Letter to the Romans:

> *For I am convinced that neither death,*
> *nor life, nor angels, nor rulers, nor*
> *things present, nor things to come,*
> *nor powers, nor height, nor depth, nor*
> *anything else in all creation, will be*
> *able to separate us from the love of God*
> *in Jesus Christ our Lord.*[9]

As we look to the eschatological horizon in which all of our human identities—including but not limited to sexuality and gender identity—no longer are of primary (or of any?) importance, we can recognize the ultimate convergence of Christian theology, queer theory, and radical love.

---

[9] Rom. 8:38–39.

Chapter One

What Is Queer Theology?

What is queer theology? For many people, "queer theology" is a troubling term. They may ask: What does theology have to do with "queerness"? Isn't "queer theology" an oxymoron or an inherent contradiction in terms? Isn't "queer" a derogatory word? For some, the word "queer" has painful connotations, especially if they were subjected to it as an epithet as a result of perceived or actual differences in sexuality or gender identity.

In recent years, however, the term "queer" has been used increasingly by scholars in a variety of theological and biblical contexts. One such example is the anthology *Queer Theology: Rethinking the Western Body*, which is a collection of provocative essays by theologians on the intersection between theology, sexuality, and gender identity.[1] Another is the groundbreaking *The Queer Bible Commentary*, a commentary on each of the books of the Christian Bible—from Genesis to Revelation—written from the perspective of those with marginalized sexualities and gender identities.[2]

So what exactly is queer theology? Simply put, if theology is defined as "talk about God" (that is, *theos* [God] + *logos* [word]), then queer theology can be understood as *queer talk about God*. This, of course, leads to the question of what exactly is meant by the term "queer," which is a more complicated issue. As such, we turn to a discussion of queer terminology.

Queer Terminology

This section will discuss at least three meanings of the word "queer": first, as an umbrella term; second, as transgressive

---

[1] See Gerard Loughlin, ed., *Queer Theology: Rethinking the Western Body* (Malden, MA: Blackwell, 2007).
[2] See Deryn Guest, Robert E. Goss, Mona West, and Thomas Bohache, eds., *The Queer Bible Commentary* (London: SCM Press, 2006).

action; and third, as erasing boundaries. Since the early 1990s, LGBT scholars (that is, scholars who have self-identified as lesbian, gay, bisexual, transgender, intersex, questioning, or allies) have reclaimed the word "queer" from its previously negative connotations.[3]

Historically, the term "queer" has been used in a negative way. For example, the *Oxford English Dictionary Online* defines "queer" as "[s]trange, odd, peculiar, eccentric" as well as "relating to homosexuals or homosexuality." The *OED Online* traces the word back as far as a 1513 translation of Virgil's *Aeneid*, and it speculates that the word is derived from the German word "quer," which means "transverse, oblique, crosswise, at right angles, obstructive."

The OED Online notes, however, that although "queer" was originally used in a derogatory sense, since the late 1980s it has been used as a "neutral or positive term," citing a 1987 newspaper article that reported on a humorous sign at a march that said "We're here because we're queer."[4] As such, we now turn to a discussion of three "neutral or positive" meanings of the word "queer."

"Queer" as Umbrella Term

One common use of the word "queer" is as an umbrella term that refers collectively to lesbian, gay, bisexual, transgender, intersex, questioning, and other individuals who identify with non-normative sexualities and/or gender identities. The term "queer" also can include "allies" who may not themselves identify as lesbian, gay, bisexual, transgender, intersex, or questioning, but stand in solidarity with their queer sisters and brothers in terms of seeking a more just world with respect to sexuality and gender identity. In other words, "queer" is a synonym for acronyms such as LGBTIQA.

It may be helpful here to review the difference between the concepts of sexuality and gender identity. Sexuality refers to the ways in which people are attracted emotionally and physically

---

[3] For a helpful discussion of the term "queer" in the context of theological education, see Carter Heyward, "We're Here, We're Queer: Teaching Sex in Seminary," in *Body and Soul: Rethinking Sexuality as Justice-Love*, ed. Marvin M. Ellison and Sylvia Thorson-Smith (Cleveland, OH: Pilgrim Press, 2003), 78–96.

[4] See "queer," *Oxford English Dictionary Online* (June 2010 draft revision), http://www.oed.com.

to the opposite sex, to the same sex, or to both sexes. Women who are primarily sexually attracted to other women are "lesbians," whereas men who are primarily sexually attracted to other men are "gay." People who are sexually attracted to both women and men are "bisexual." People who are sexually attracted to people of the opposite sex are "straight" or "heterosexual." In general, people within the LGBT community prefer the terms "lesbian," "gay," and "bisexual" to the more clinical term "homosexual."

By contrast, gender identity refers to the ways in which people self-identify with respect to their genders ("female" or "male"), regardless of the sex that they were assigned at birth. People who identify with a gender that is different from their assigned sex at birth are "transgender." Such people may or may not have had medical treatment (for example, hormones or surgery) to align their physical bodies with their gender identities. By contrast, people who identify with a gender that is aligned with their birth sex are "cisgender." People who decline to identify with one gender or the other are "gender queer." Finally, people who are born with ambiguous genitalia or genitalia of both sexes are "intersex."[5]

It is important to note that gender identity is a concept that is distinct from sexuality. In other words, the fact that a person is transgender is separate from that person's sexuality. Thus, a trans woman (that is, a person who was assigned the male sex at birth but who is self-identified as female) may be a lesbian (that is, sexually attracted to other female-identified people), heterosexual (that is, sexually attracted to male-identified people), or bisexual (that is, sexually attracted to both female-identified and male-identified people).

To summarize, the term "queer" is often used as an umbrella or collective term to describe people with marginalized sexualities (lesbian, gay, or bisexual) as well as with marginalized gender identities (transgender) or genitalia (intersex). We see

---

[5] For additional resources about transgender issues, see Susannah Cornwall, "'State of Mind' versus 'Concrete Set of Facts': The Contrasting of Transgender and Intersex in Church Documents on Sexuality," *Theology and Sexuality* 15, no. 1 (Jan. 2009): 7–28; Joanne Herman, *Transgender Explained for Those Who Are Not* (Bloomington, IN: AuthorHouse, 2009); Victoria S. Kolakowski, "Toward a Christian Ethical Response to Transsexual Persons," *Theology and Sexuality* no. 6 (March 1997): 10–31; Susan Stryker, *Transgender History* (Berkeley, CA: Seal Press, 2008).

this use of the word "queer" as an umbrella or collective term in the works of LGBT theologians such as Nancy Wilson, the current moderator of the Metropolitan Community Churches,[6] and the late Robert Williams, one of the first openly gay priests in the Episcopal Church.[7]

"Queer" as Transgressive Action

In addition to the umbrella sense of the word "queer," there is a second meaning of "queer" that is an intentional reclaiming of a word that previously had only negative connotations. In recent years, the word "queer" has been used by many LGBT people as positive label that proudly embraces all that is transgressive or opposed to societal norms, particularly with respect to sexuality and gender identity. This use parallels the reclaiming of the word "black" by African Americans during the 1960s as a positive term of pride. Prior to that time, the preferred term was "colored" or "negro," since "black" had a negative connotation in a racial context.

The use of the word "queer" as a positive term of pride for LGBT people can be traced as far back as the late 1980s. The *Oxford English Dictionary Online* cites a 1989 article that describes the LGBT community as a "queer nation" that is "assertively coed, multi-racial and anti-consumerist."[8] In 1990, the radical organization Queer Nation was founded with the goal of fighting anti-LGBT violence and prejudice through activism and confrontational tactics such as outing closeted politicians and celebrities. Queer Nation has used a number of slogans including "We're here, we're queer, get used to it!" and "Out of the closets and into the streets!"

Along these lines, Robert Shore-Goss, an openly gay theologian and minister with the Metropolitan Community Churches, has described queer theology as a fundamentally transgressive enterprise in his book *Queering Christ: Beyond Jesus Acted Up*. Indeed, Shore-Goss has argued that transgression should

---

[6] See Nancy Wilson, *Our Tribe: Queer Folks, God, Jesus, and the Bible* (San Francisco, HarperSanFrancisco, 1995), 231–80 (outlining a "queer" theology of sexuality that is grounded in "promiscuous hospitality").

[7] See Robert Williams, *Just as I Am: A Practical Guide to Being Out, Proud, and Christian* (New York: HarperPerennial, 1992), xxv (explaining his decision to use "queer" instead of "gay" or "gay and lesbian").

[8] See "Queer Nation," *Oxford English Dictionary Online* (December 2007 draft entry), http://www.oed.com.

be seen as a central metaphor for queer theologies. For Shore-Goss, the term "queer" is used to describe an action that "turns upside down, inside out" that which is seen as normative, including "heteronormative theologies." In that sense, the act of queering traditional theological discourse has a "prophetic edge."[9]

Thus, the second meaning of "queer" is a self-conscious embrace of all that is transgressive of societal norms, particularly in the context of sexuality and gender identity. In fact, this term is best understood as a verb or an action. That is, to "queer" something is to engage with a methodology that challenges and disrupts the status quo. Like the function of the court jester or the subversive traditions of Mardi Gras, to "queer" something is to turn convention and authority on its head. It is about seeing things in a different light and reclaiming voices and sources that previously had been ignored, silenced, or discarded. It is proudly asserting a worldview for which LGBT people have been historically taunted, condemned, beaten, tortured, and killed.

"Queer" as Erasing Boundaries

A third meaning of "queer" is grounded in the academic discipline known as queer theory, which arose in the early 1990s and is indebted to the work of the late French philosopher Michel Foucault. Put simply, queer theory views sexuality as something that is "continually undergoing negotiation and dissemination, rather than as a mere natural (let alone medical) fact."[10] In other words, queer theory challenges and disrupts the traditional notions that sexuality and gender identity are simply questions of scientific fact or that such concepts can be reduced to fixed binary categories such as "homosexual" vs. "heterosexual" or "female" vs. "male." As such, this third definition of "queer" refers to the erasing or deconstructing of boundaries with respect to these categories of sexuality and gender.

In other words, queer theory argues that the significance of

---

[9] Robert E. Goss, *Queering Christ: Beyond Jesus Acted Up* (Cleveland, OH: Pilgrim Press, 2002), 228–29.
[10] Andrew Edgar and Peter Sedgwick, *Cultural Theory: The Key Concepts*, 2nd ed. (London: Routledge, 2008), 277.

traditional categories of sexuality and gender identity are actually social constructions. For example, Foucault demonstrated how the term "homosexual" was only invented in the late nineteenth century in Germany. This is not to say that there weren't people engaging in same-sex acts prior to that time. In fact, there certainly have been people engaged in same-sex acts throughout history and across cultures. What Foucault was saying, however, was that this was the first time that a person's *identity* was defined or categorized in terms of the gender of her or his preferred sexual partner(s). Thus, sexuality became an issue of *being*—that is, *who* one was—as opposed to *what* one was doing.

Although in some ways it may be helpful for a minority group (such as "homosexuals") to identify itself in essentialist terms for purposes of achieving greater political or legal power, ultimately such classifications are problematic because, as Foucault pointed out, such classifications are actually a means by which society circumscribes and exercises power and control over the classified group.

For example, we could imagine a world that limits marriage to people who only have a hat size less than 7½ or only people who prefer Pepsi over Coke. In such a world, such classifications—that is, one's hat size or preferred brand of soda—would have significant consequences for its inhabitants. However, these classifications are no less "natural" than classifying people on the basis of the gender of their preferred sex partners. For example, for much of history, people were classified in terms of whether they were the penetrators (tops) or the penetrated (bottoms) in sexual acts, and not by the gender of their preferred sex partners."[11]

As such, categories of sexuality are ultimately social constructions. Furthermore, the fact that sexualities are traditionally reduced to the binaries of "homosexuality" vs. "heterosexuality" ignores the more complicated notion that sexuality occurs across a spectrum. Indeed, the existence of bisexual people is a challenge for straight people as well as lesbians and

---

[11] See Martti Nissinen, *Homoeroticism in the Biblical World: A Historical Perspective* (Minneapolis, MN: Fortress Press, 1998), 128–34 ("The Interpretation of Same-Sex Relations Then and Now").

gay men because it threatens the neat categories of "homosexuality" vs. "heterosexuality."

The same analysis applies to gender identity. The existence of transgender and intersex people challenges the traditional binary categorization of gender and sex as "female" vs. "male." This is precisely why cross-dressing can be troubling for many people; it threatens our society's neat, socially constructed notions of gender expression and sex. As Judith Butler has argued, gender is a performative act as opposed to a matter of essentialism or nature. That is, gendered notions of "femaleness" and "maleness" are culturally constructed and are not necessarily related to one's biological sex. Thus, whenever a person refuses to engage in the "correct" gender expression that is expected of her or his biological sex (such as in the case of cross-dressing), this threatens the social order and, as such, reveals the socially constructed nature of gender identity.[12]

Gerard Loughlin, an openly gay theologian at the University of Durham, has described "queer" as that which "seeks to outwit identity." In other words, "queer" destabilizes that which is perceived as "normal" identity—for example, the binary choice between "heterosexuality" and "homosexuality"—by erasing the boundaries between such polarities and thus symbolizing a "difference, a divergence." For Loughlin, queer theory is a means by which "heteropatriarchal Christianity" can be destabilized and deconstructed.[13]

Thus, the third meaning of "queer" is the erasing or deconstructing of boundaries, particularly with respect to the essentialist or fixed binary categories of sexuality and gender. As we have seen, this meaning of "queer" is grounded in the academic fields of queer studies and queer theory, which in turn is based upon the work of academics such as Michel Foucault, Judith Butler, and Eve Kosofsky Sedgwick.

---

[12] For a discussion of Butler's work in the context of religious studies, see Ellen T. Armour and Susan M. St. Ville, eds., *Bodily Citations: Religion and Judith Butler* (New York: Columbia University Press, 2006).
[13] Gerard Loughlin, "Introduction: The End of Sex," in Louglin, *Queer Theology*, 9–10.

Defining Queer Theology

So what exactly is queer theology? If theology is "talk about God," then, in light of the above three definitions of "queer," there are at least three possible definitions for "queer theology." First, queer theology is LGBT people "talking about God." Second, queer theology is "talking about God" in a self-consciously transgressive manner, especially in terms of challenging societal norms about sexuality and gender. Third, queer theology is "talk about God" that challenges and deconstructs the natural binary categories of sexual and gender identity. Let us examine each of these three definitions in turn.

First, in light of the umbrella or collective term definition of "queer," queer theology can be understood as LGBT people "talking about God." In other words, queer theology is a short-hand term for theology that is done by and for LGBT people. Thus, instead of writing the phrase "talk about God by and for lesbian, gay, bisexual, transgender, intersex, questioning people as well as our allies" over and over again, we can simply use the term "queer theology" as shorthand. As we have seen, Nancy Wilson has articulated what she calls a "queer theology of sexuality" that is grounded in bodily hospitality. For Wilson, this queer theology speaks to gay men, lesbians, bisexual people, and others who identify as "queer."[14]

Second, in light of the definition of "queer" as transgression, queer theology can be understood as a theological method that is self-consciously transgressive, especially by challenging societal norms about sexuality and gender. Thus, queer theology refers to a way of doing theology that, in the words of the *Magnificat*, brings down the powerful and lifts up the lowly.[15] In particular, this theology seeks to unearth silenced voices or hidden perspectives. One example of this kind of theology is the "indecent theology" of the late bisexual theologian Marcella Althaus-Reid from the University of Edinburgh. According to Althaus-Reid, queer theology should shock people out of their complacency and help them see theology in a new light.

---

[14] Wilson, *Our Tribe*, 231–80.
[15] See Luke 1:52.

Althaus-Reid certainly did that in her books *Indecent Theology* and *The Queer God*, which contained provocative chapters such as "Oral Sex: sexual his/torias in oral theology"[16] and "Kneeling: deviant theologians."[17] Hence, queer theology differs from prophetic discourse in that queer theology is self-consciously transgressive in terms of methodology, whereas prophetic discourse involves speaking on behalf of the divine and subordinating one's will to that of God (which, of course, may also be a transgressive act).

Third, in light of the definition of "queer" as erasing boundaries, queer theology can be understood as a way of doing theology that is rooted in queer theory and that critiques the binary categories of sexuality (that is, homosexual vs. heterosexual) and gender identity (that is, female vs. male) as socially constructed. In other words, queer theology argues that the discourse of classical Christian theology ultimately requires the erasing of the boundaries of essentialist categories of not only sexuality and gender identity, but also more fundamental boundaries such as life vs. death, and divine vs. human. The recent work of the openly lesbian theologian Elizabeth Stuart of the University of Winchester on the eschatological dimension of the sacraments (such as baptism and the Eucharist) is strongly rooted in this view of queer theology.[18]

While this book will draw upon all three definitions of queer theology, the main focus will be on the third definition: that is, how queer theology, like queer studies and queer theory, erases boundaries by challenging and deconstructing the "natural" binary categories of sexual and gender identity. Indeed, it is the thesis of this book that Christian theology itself is a fundamentally queer enterprise because it also challenges and deconstructs—through radical love—all kinds of binary categories that on the surface seem fixed and unchangeable (such as life vs. death, or divine vs. human), but that ultimately are fluid and malleable.

---

[16] Marcella Althaus-Reid, *Indecent Theology: Theological Perversions in Sex, Gender and Politics* (London: Routledge, 2000), 134.

[17] Marcella Althaus-Reid, *The Queer God* (London: Routledge, 2003), 7.

[18] See Elizabeth Stuart, "Making No Sense: Liturgy as Queer Space," in Isherwood and Jordan, *Dancing Theology in Fetish Boots*, 113–23; Elizabeth Stuart, "The Priest at the Altar: The Eucharistic Erasure of Sex," in Althaus-Reid and Isherwood, *Trans/formations*, 127–38; Elizabeth Stuart, "Sacramental Flesh," in Loughlin, *Queer Theology*, 65–75.

In other words, Christian theology is fundamentally a queer enterprise because it focuses upon the incarnation, life, death, resurrection, ascension, and second coming of Jesus Christ, all of which are events that turn upside down our traditional understanding of life and death, divine and human, center and margins, beginnings and endings, infinite and finite, and punishment and forgiveness. As with the case of queer theory, it is in Jesus Christ that all of these seemingly fixed binary categories are ultimately challenged and collapsed.

Four Sources of Queer Theology

Where did queer theology come from? Did it just fall out of the sky? Was it an invention of LGBT activists? For many people, the notion of queer theology is an oxymoron, particularly in light of how traditional Christianity has condemned—and continues to condemn—same-sex acts and gender-variant identities as intrinsically sinful. However, in recent years an increasing number of theologians have written about queer theology, drawing upon a variety of different theological sources.[19]

Like all other theologies, queer theology draws upon at least four sources: (1) scripture, (2) tradition, (3) reason, and (4) experience. This multiplicity of sources is important because, on the one hand, theology has never been simply about reading the Bible literally (that is, scripture) nor simply about what the church authorities have taught (that is, tradition). On the other hand, theology has never been simply a matter of drawing upon philosophy (that is, reason) nor has it simply been equated with the human experience of the divine (that is, experience).

Rather, theology is a synthesis of all four sources, and each of these sources acts as a "check and balance" for the other three. Of course, different traditions give different weight for each of these sources. For example, evangelical Protestants rely heavily upon scripture, Roman Catholics rely heavily upon tradition, Anglicans rely heavily upon reason, and progressive

---

[19] See e.g., Loughlin, *Queer Theology*; Althaus-Reid and Isherwood, *Trans/formations*.

Protestants rely heavily upon experience. But it is important to realize that each of these sources must still be read in light of the other three. Let us now turn to each of these four sources in the context of queer theology.

Queer Scripture

First, queer theology draws upon scripture—that is, the Hebrew and Christian scriptures (also known as the First and Second Testaments)—in creative ways. Although scripture (and, in particular, the handful of "texts of terror"[20] for LGBT people) traditionally has been used as a means of oppressing LGBT people, queer biblical scholars in recent years have not only countered these antiqueer readings with alternative readings, but they have also "taken back" or "reclaimed" the Bible by interpreting it positively and constructively from their own perspectives.

For example, take the story of Sodom and Gomorrah in Genesis 19, which has been the paradigmatic story for God's punishment of same-sex acts. In that story, two angelic visitors stay overnight in the town of Sodom. However, the lawless men of Sodom demand that the visitors' host, Lot, turn the visitors over so that they may "know" them. The visitors escape along with Lot's family, and God destroys Sodom and its sister city, Gomorrah, with fire and brimstone.[21]

Although the story of Sodom and Gomorrah has been interpreted traditionally as evidence of God's punishment of LGBT people, queer biblical scholars have argued that the story is actually a condemnation of the sin of *inhospitality* toward strangers, which had life or death consequences in the harsh desert environment of the biblical world. This is evidenced by the descriptions of Sodom and Gomorrah elsewhere in the Bible (for example, Ezekiel 16:48–49), which focus on inhospitality instead of same-sex acts.[22]

Ironically, some LGBT theologians and ethicists such as

[20] See Phyllis Trible, *Texts of Terror: Literary-Feminist Readings of Biblical Narratives* (Philadelphia, PA: Fortress Press, 1984).
[21] See generally Gen. 19.
[22] See Daniel A. Helminiak, *What the Bible Really Says About Homosexuality*, millennium ed. (Tajique, NM: Alamo Square Press), 43–50.

Nancy Wilson and Kathy Rudy have "queered" the Sodom narrative by placing hospitality at the *center* of queer theological reflection. For example, Wilson has constructed a "queer theology of sexuality" by focusing on the gift of "promiscuous" or "bodily hospitality" that many LGBT people have.[23] Rudy, an openly lesbian ethicist at Duke University, has suggested that nonmonogamous sex acts—including anonymous and communal sex—can be viewed in terms of a progressive ethic of hospitality.[24]

Much has been written about the debate over the meaning of the half-dozen or so LBGT "texts of terror" in the Bible, and I will not rehearse those arguments here.[25] However, it is important to note that queer theologians have gone beyond these "texts of terror" and have read the Bible in creative and constructive ways as a means of affirming LGBT experience.[26] For example, Nancy Wilson has argued that LGBT people can be found in a number of biblical narratives—including David and Jonathan, Ruth and Naomi, the Roman Centurion, the Ethiopian Eunuch, and Mary, Martha, and Lazarus—which she refers to as "our gay and lesbian tribal texts."[27]

In 2006, over thirty LGBT religious scholars, ministers, and writers contributed to *The Queer Bible Commentary*, which was the first queer commentary on all the books of the Hebrew and Christian scriptures, from Genesis to Revelation. As the preface states, the commentary shows that biblical texts have the "ever-surprising capacity to be disruptive, unsettling and

---

[23] Wilson, *Our Tribe*, 231–80.
[24] See Kathy Rudy, *Sex and the Church: Gender Homosexuality, and the Transformation of Christian Ethics* (Boston: Beacon Press, 1997), 108–30.
[25] For a description of the standard LGBT "texts of terror" (that is, Gen. 19, Lev. 18:22, Lev. 20:13, Deut. 22:5, Deut. 23:1, Rom. 1:26–27, 1 Cor. 6:9, and 1 Tim. 1:10) and responses by LGBT theologians, see Helminiak, *What the Bible Really Says About Homosexuality*; Goss, *Queering Christ*, 185–220; Justin Tanis, *Trans-Gendered: Theology, Ministry, and Communities of Faith* (Cleveland, OH: Pilgrim Press, 2003), 55–84 (transgender passages); Sally Gross, "Intersexuality and Scripture," *Theology and Sexuality* 11 (September 1999): 65–74 (intersex passages). Other resources include L. William Countryman, *Dirt, Greed and Sex: Sexual Ethics in the New Testament and Their Implications for Today* (Philadelphia, PA: Fortress Press, 1988); Peter J. Gomes, *The Good Book: Reading the Bible with Mind and Heart* (San Francisco: HarperSanFrancisco, 1996), 144–72; D.J. Good, "Reading Strategies for Biblical Passages on Same-Sex Relations," *Theology and Sexuality*, no. 7 (Sept. 1997): 70–82; and Mark D. Jordan, *The Ethics of Sex* (Oxford, UK: Blackwell Publishers, 2002). For a helpful resource for LGBT people who are recovering from the abusive use of the Bible, see Rembert Truluck, *Steps to Recovery from Bible Abuse* (Gaithersburg, MD: Chi Rho Press, 2000).
[26] For discussions about queer hermeneutics, see Timothy R. Koch, "A Homoerotic Approach to Scripture," *Theology and Sexuality*, no. 14 (Jan. 2001): 10–22; Mona West, "Reading the Bible as Queer Americans: Social Location and the Hebrew Scriptures," *Theology and Sexuality*, no. 10 (March 1999): 28–42.
[27] See Wilson, *Our Tribe*, 111–64. Texts cited by Wilson include 1 Sam. 18:1–4, 20:14–17 (Jonathan and David); Ruth 1:16–17 (Ruth and Naomi); Matt. 8:5–13, Luke 7:1–10 (the Roman Centurion); Acts 8:26–40 (the Ethiopian Eunuch); John 11 (Mary, Martha, and Lazarus).

unexpectedly but delightfully *queer*." Furthermore, the contrib-
utors employed a wide range of hermeneutic approaches,
including "feminist, queer, deconstructionist, postcolonial,
and utopian theories, the social sciences, and historical-critical
discourses."[28]

Other examples of using scripture as a positive source for
queer theology include: *Jacob's Wound: Homoerotic Narrative in
the Literature of Ancient Israel; Queer Commentary and the Hebrew
Bible; The Subversive Gospel: A New Testament Commentary of
Liberation; Take Back the Word: A Queer Reading of the Bible;
Torah Queeries: Weekly Commentaries on the Hebrew Bible; When
Deborah Met Jael: Lesbian Biblical Hermeneutics;* and *The Word
Is Out: Daily Reflections on the Bible for Lesbians and Gay Men.*[29]
By engaging with scripture from our unique social locations,
queer people are able to articulate more clearly how the Word
of God has touched us, and how we in turn can "talk about
God" from an authentically queer perspective.

Queer Tradition

Queer theology draws upon tradition—that is, church
history as well as the teachings of the church over the last
two millennia—in creative ways. As in the case of scripture,
Christian tradition usually has been seen as being uniformly
anti-queer. However, in 1955 Derrick Sherwin Bailey, an
Anglican priest, published the groundbreaking historical study
Homosexuality and the Western Christian Tradition, which for
the first time challenged the traditionally negative view of the
Christian theological tradition toward LGBT people.[30]

Bailey's book was followed twenty-five years later by
*Christianity, Social Tolerance, and Homosexuality: Gay People in
Western Europe from the Beginning of the Christian Era to the
Fourteenth Century*, a groundbreaking work by the late John

---

[28] Guest et al., *Queer Bible Commentary*, xiii.

[29] See Theodore W. Jennings, *Jacob's Wound: Homoerotic Narrative in the Literature of Ancient Israel* (New York: Continuum, 2005); Ken Stone, ed., *Queer Commentary and the Hebrew Bible* (Cleveland, OH: Pilgrim Press, 2001); Tom Hanks, *The Subversive Gospel: A New Testament Commentary of Liberation* (Cleveland, OH: Pilgrim Press, 2000); Robert E. Goss and Mona West, eds., *Take Back the Word: A Queer Reading of the Bible* (Cleveland, OH: Pilgrim Press, 2000); Drinkwater et al., *Torah Queeries*; Deryn Guest, *When Deborah Met Jael: Lesbian Biblical Hermeneutics* (London: SCM Press, 2005); and Chris Glaser, *The Word Is Out: Daily Reflections on the Bible for Lesbians and Gay Men* (Louisville, KY: Westminster John Knox Press, 1994).

[30] See Derrick Sherwin Bailey, *Homosexuality and the Western Christian Tradition* (London: Longmans, Green, 1955), viii.

Boswell, an openly gay history professor at Yale University. Boswell argued that Christianity was not uniformly homophobic throughout its early history and that it only became significantly homophobic in the twelfth and thirteenth centuries.[31] The book was incredibly influential and even generated a collection of essays on its impact on religious scholarship.[32] Prior to his death in 1994, Boswell published *Same-Sex Unions in Premodern Europe*, which argued that same-sex blessing rites existed in the Christian church for centuries.[33]

In addition to Boswell, other scholars have reexamined the Christian tradition from the LGBT perspective. These include Bernadette Brooten, a religious studies professor at Brandeis University, who wrote about female homoeroticism in early Christianity—an issue that was largely overlooked by Boswell—in *Love Between Women: Early Christian Responses to Female Homoeroticism*, and Judith C. Brown, who documented the story of Sister Benedetta Carlini, a lesbian abbess in sixteenth-century Italy, in *Immodest Acts: The Life of a Lesbian Nun in Renaissance Italy*.[34]

Finally, a number of LGBT scholars have reexamined the work of classical theologians from a queer perspective. These include Mark D. Jordan, an openly gay theologian at Harvard Divinity School, who examined the work of medieval theologians such as Peter Damian and Thomas Aquinas in *The Invention of Sodomy in Christian Theology*. Jordan concluded that the theological term "sodomy" was invented by medieval theologians as a result of their fear of the pure erotic state (that is, sexual pleasure without any connection to biological reproduction) and thus created a category by which such a state could be condemned unequivocally by the church.[35]

Such scholars also include Virginia Burrus, a professor of early church history at Drew University, who has read early

---

[31] See John Boswell, *Christianity, Social Tolerance, and Homosexuality: Gay People in Western Europe from the Beginning of the Christian Era to the Fourteenth Century* (Chicago: University of Chicago Press, 1980).

[32] See Mathew Kuefler, ed., *The Boswell Thesis: Essays on Christianity, Social Tolerance, and Homosexuality* (Chicago: University of Chicago Press, 2006).

[33] See John Boswell, *Same-Sex Unions in Premodern Europe* (New York: Vintage Books, 1994).

[34] See Bernadette J. Brooten, *Love Between Women: Early Christian Responses to Female Homoeroticism* (Chicago: University of Chicago Press, 1996); Judith C. Brown, *Immodest Acts: The Life of a Lesbian Nun in Renaissance Italy* (New York: Oxford University Press, 1988).

[35] See Mark D. Jordan, *The Invention of Sodomy in Christian Theology* (Chicago: University of Chicago Press, 1997).

Christian stories of saints from a variety of interpretive lenses, including queer theory, in *The Sex Lives of Saints: An Erotics of Ancient Hagiography*, and who, along with Mark Jordan and Karmen MacKendrick, has examined the themes of seduction and confession in the work of Augustine of Hippo in *Seducing Augustine: Bodies, Desires, Confessions*.[36]

By reclaiming the Christian tradition, these queer scholars have located the LGBT experience squarely within the history and teachings of the church. As such, we are able to draw upon this work as a source for constructing our own theologies.

Queer Reason

Queer theology also draws upon reason—that is, our ability as human beings to observe the world and use philosophy to know God. Traditionally speaking, this source of theology assumes that God can be known by observing nature and the created order. For example, Thomas Aquinas' famous five proofs for God are derived from the principles of reason.

Traditionally speaking, reason has not been seen as a queer-friendly source of theology. This is due in large part to the Roman Catholic view that nonprocreative sexual acts (including same-sex acts) are always intrinsically evil as a matter of natural law. However, the Roman Catholic theologian Gareth Moore challenged this traditional view in his book *A Question of Truth: Christianity and Homosexuality*. According to Moore, the magisterium of the Roman Catholic Church must ask itself whether what it teaches is actually true. Is it really true that all same-sex acts and relationships are intrinsically evil? Is it true that all LGBT people are unhappy and poorly adjusted? Is it true that same-sex acts and relationships do not occur naturally in the created order?[37]

The truth is that, contrary to the teachings of the Roman Catholic Church, there are hundreds of animal and bird species in the natural world that engage in same-sex acts or gender-variant behavior.[38] Furthermore, there have been numerous

---

[36] See Virginia Burrus, *The Sex Lives of Saints: An Erotics of Ancient Hagiography* (Philadelphia: University of Pennsylvania Press, 2004); Burrus et al., *Seducing Augustine*.

[37] See Gareth Moore, *A Question of Truth: Christianity and Homosexuality* (London: Continuum, 2003), 27–37.

[38] See Bruce Bagemihl, *Biological Exuberance: Animal Homosexuality and Natural Diversity* (New York: St. Martin's Press, 1999).

Roman Catholic bishops, priests, members of religious orders, and laypersons who have come out of the closet and written about their experiences as LGBT people.[39]

After reviewing the scientific evidence, Moore concludes in his book that the "only rational course at the moment" is to "continue to believe in the possible goodness of homosexual relationships." For Moore, this is not a question of dissent, but rather the fact that the Roman Catholic Church currently lacks any sound arguments upon which its condemnation of same-sex acts can be based. That is, "the church teaches badly."[40]

In addition to challenging the traditional natural law arguments about the intrinsically evil nature of same-sex acts,[41] queer theologians have increasingly drawn upon reason in the form of poststructuralist philosophy—that is, queer theory— in constructing their queer theology. Queer theory rejects the traditional view that categories of sexuality (that is, homosexual vs. heterosexual) and gender identity (that is, female vs. male) are "natural," essentialist, or fixed. Instead, as articulated in the work of theorists such as Judith Butler and Michel Foucault, queer theory argues that the meanings of such categories are socially constructed.

This is not to deny that there are in fact physiological differences between people in terms of sexual attraction and bodies. These differences *do* exist. Furthermore, this is not to deny that sexuality and gender identity can effectively be immutable characteristics for many people and thus are deserving of legal protections akin to race. However, the *significance* of such differences in terms of sexuality and gender identity is not simply a matter of "nature," but rather is socially constructed. As noted above, even though people may differ in terms of, say, hat size, that particular physical marker of difference has little to no

---

[39] See, e.g., Rembert G. Weakland, *A Pilgrim in a Pilgrim Church: Memoirs of a Catholic Archbishop* (Grand Rapids, MI: William B. Eerdmans Publishing, 2009); Robert L. Arpin, *Wonderfully, Fearfully Made: Letters on Living with Hope, Teaching Understanding, and Ministering with Love, from a Gay Catholic Priest with AIDS* (San Francisco: HarperSanFrancisco, 1993); Paul Murray, *Life in Paradox: The Story of a Gay Catholic Priest* (Winchester UK: O Books, 2008); Amie M. Evans and Trebor Healey, eds., *Queer and Catholic* (New York: Routledge, 2008); Dugan McGinley, *Acts of Faith, Acts of Love: Gay Catholic Autobiographies as Sacred Texts* (New York: Continuum, 2004); Scott Pomfret, *Since My Last Confession: A Gay Catholic Memoir* (New York: Arcade Publishing, 2008).

[40] Moore, *A Question of Truth*, 282.

[41] For a discussion on moral argumentation and homosexuality, see Pim Pronk, *Against Nature?: Types of Moral Argumentation Regarding Homosexuality* (Grand Rapids, MI: William B. Eerdmans Publishing, 1993).

relevance in everyday life. Similarly, there is no reason why a person's genitalia must *automatically* determine everything from hair and clothing styles to preferred color (for example, pink vs. blue) to family role to career choices. It is important to understand that the spectrum of behaviors normally associated with an individual's birth-assigned sex are actually a matter of a social convention that is constantly changing.

Queer theologians have used queer theory to challenge not only the fluidity of sexual and gender boundaries,[42] but also the boundaries relating to Christian theology itself. These boundaries include the divine vs. human, soul vs. body, life vs. death, heaven vs. earth, center vs. margins, and numerous other boundaries that are dissolved or erased by radical love as we approach the eschatological horizon. Indeed, Christian theology is, as I have suggested, fundamentally a queer enterprise.

Finally, queer theologians—and especially queer theologians of color—are drawing upon other forms of reason and philosophy, such as a postcolonial theory, in their "talk about God." The language of postcolonial theory is especially effective in terms of dealing with issues of hybridity and intersectionality (that is, the multiple social locations of sexuality, gender identity, sex, race, and other identities) and the power dynamics between and within various identity groups.[43]

Queer Experience

Finally, queer theology draws upon experience as a source for theology. As in the case of other contextual theologies, queer theology is premised upon the belief that God acts within the specific contexts of our lives and experiences, despite the fact that LGBT lives and experiences have been excluded from traditional theological discourse. Indeed, queer experience is an important—if not critical—source for doing theology from a queer perspective.

---

[42] For the intersection of queer theory with religious studies, see Armour and St. Ville, *Bodily Citations*; James Bernauer and Jeremy Carrette, eds., *Michel Foucault and Theology: The Politics of Religious Experience* (Aldershot, UK: Ashgate, 2004); Jeremy R. Carrette, *Foucault and Religion: Spiritual Corporality and Political Spirituality* (London: Routledge, 2000).

[43] For examples of postcolonial readings of classical theologians, see Kwok Pui-lan, Don H. Compier, and Joerg Rieger, eds., *Empire and the Christian Tradition: New Readings of Classical Theologians* (Minneapolis, MN: Fortress Press, 2007).

In recent years, there have been a number of anthologies of the voices of LGBT people of faith, including *From Queer to Eternity: Spirituality in the Lives of Lesbian, Gay and Bisexual People*; *Recreations: Religion and Spirituality in the Lives of Queer People*; *Queer and Catholic*; and *Sanctified: An Anthology of Poetry by LGBT Christians*.[44] These anthologies are helpful sources in terms of articulating experience as a source for queer theology.

Queer theologians of all backgrounds and perspectives have used experience as a source of theology. For example, Robert Shore-Goss has written provocatively about his erotic love for Jesus in constructing a queer christology. Shore-Goss tells us that, while a novice with the Jesuits, he imagined a "naked Jesus as a muscular, handsome, bearded man." Shore-Goss wrote that, later on, during "passionate lovemaking, I felt Christ in a way that I only experienced in my solitary erotic prayer."[45]

Carter Heyward, an openly lesbian theologian and professor *emerita* at the Episcopal Divinity School—and one of the first female priests in the Episcopal Church and the wider Anglican Communion—has written about finding God in her sensual and embodied connection with nature while walking with her dogs. She writes that, in observing the "trees' gnarled roots at the water's edge, the wind-chill whipping my cheeks, the pile of dog shit I step in, the crows harping from the fence, the joggers and other walkers," she knows that her sensuality is her "most common link" to the rest of the earth and "can be trusted."[46]

Laurel Dykstra, an openly bisexual theologian and member of the Catholic Worker movement, has written about how, as "a Canadian living in the United States, a bisexual person, [and] a theologically educated lay person," she is always living in "in-between spaces." As such, her sexuality and spiritually are closely connected. Indeed, Dykstra's in-between experience

---

[44] See Peter Sweasey, *From Queer to Eternity: Spirituality in the Lives of Lesbian, Gay and Bisexual People* (London: Cassell, 1997); Catherine Lake, ed., *Recreations: Religion and Spirituality in the Lives of Queer People* (Toronto: Queer Press, 1999); Evans and Healey, *Queer and Catholic*; Justin R. Cannon, *Sanctified: An Anthology of Poetry by LGBT Christians* (Scotts Valley, CA: Createspace, 2008).

[45] Robert E. Goss, "Passionate Love for Christ: Out of the Closet, Into the Streets," in *Male Lust: Pleasure, Power, and Transformation*, ed. Kerwin Kay, Jill Nagle, and Baruch Gould (Binghamton, NY: Harrington Park Press, 2000), 298, 301.

[46] Carter Heyward, *Touching Our Strength: The Erotic as Power and the Love of God* (San Francisco: HarperSanFrancisco, 1989), 93.

actually helps her to "live and love joyfully and defiantly, like Jesus embracing the glorious ambiguity and refusing to be held by purity codes, gay or straight."[47]

Finally, Justin Tanis, a self-identified transman and ordained Metropolitan Community Church minister, has written about how his theological work arises out of the intersections of his personal experiences as a "transsexual person" and his "professional life as a clergyperson." Tanis described how his calling in terms of gender was "remarkably familiar to me; it was like my experience of discerning a call to the ministry." Like his vocational call, the journey of transitioning for Tanis was a "journey to authenticity, a deeply spiritual process."[48]

By writing about their experiences of encountering God within their particular social contexts, each of the above queer theologians have shown that experience is a central source for "talking about God" and doing queer theology.

Example: Same-Sex Marriage as Sacrament?

This chapter will close with an example of "doing" queer theology in light of the four sources of theology described above. Specifically, it examines the issue of same-sex marriages and whether such marriages should be treated as a sacrament (that is, a formal rite of the church) in the same way as opposite-sex marriages.[49] This, of course, is an issue that is creating much division in the mainline Christian churches, particularly as more civil jurisdictions in the United States (for example, Connecticut, Iowa, Massachusetts, New Hampshire, and Vermont) permit same-sex couples to marry under civil law.

With respect to the first source—scripture—a queer theologian might turn to narratives in the Bible about intimate same-sex relationships, including Jonathan and David (who made a "covenant" together),[50] Ruth and Naomi (whose vow to

---

[47] Laurel Dykstra, "Jesus, Bread, Wine and Roses: A Bisexual Feminist at the Catholic Worker," in *Blessed Bi Spirit: Bisexual People of Faith*, ed. Debra R. Kolodny (New York: Continuum, 2000), 78–79, 87.

[48] Tanis, *Trans-Gendered*, 1, 4.

[49] It should be noted that the Roman Catholic Church recognizes seven sacraments, including marriage, but most Protestant denominations recognize only two sacraments: baptism and Eucharist. Here, I use the term "sacrament" broadly as a formal rite of the church.

[50] See 1 Sam. 20:16.

follow each other is traditionally used in opposite-sex marriage ceremonies),[51] and even Jesus and the Beloved Disciple. Nancy Wilson has written about these same-sex relationships,[52] as has Robert Williams, who hypothesized that Jesus was gay and that the Beloved Disciple was not only his lover but also another name for Lazarus.[53]

With respect to the second source—tradition—a queer theologian might draw from John Boswell's work on same-sex rites of blessing throughout the history of the church. Boswell hypothesized that these rites were based upon ancient Roman "brotherhood" rites and arose out of an early Christian fascination with same-sex saint couples, including "military pairs like Serg[ius] and Bacchus" who may have been in romantic relationships.[54] Similarly, such a theologian could draw upon the research of Alan Bray, a University of London historian, which focused on an Anglican tradition—dating back to at least the fourteenth century—of burying two same-sex friends, complete with marital imagery, in the same tomb.[55]

With respect to the third source—reason—a queer theologian might turn to queer theory and poststructuralist thought to challenge the notion that, as a result of "nature," marriage must be restricted to one man and one woman. As noted above, there are hundreds of animal species that engage in same-sex acts and gender-variant behaviors. Also, as in the case of sexuality and gender identity, the definitional boundaries with respect to marriage are socially constructed and do change over time.[56] For example, polygamy was recognized in biblical times, and the antimiscegenation laws that prohibited interracial marriage were not declared unconstitutional by the U.S. Supreme Court until 1967.

---

[51] See Ruth 1:16.
[52] See Wilson, *Our Tribe*, 140–57.
[53] Williams, *Just As I Am*, 120–23.
[54] Boswell, *Same-Sex Unions in Premodern Europe*, 218–19.
[55] See Alan Bray, *The Friend* (Chicago: University of Chicago Press, 2003); see also Alan Bray, "Friendship, the Family and Liturgy: A Rite for Blessing Friendship in Traditional Christianity," *Theology and Sexuality*, no. 13 (Sept. 2000): 15–33. For example, Blessed John Henry Cardinal Newman was buried in the same grave as his close friend Ambrose St. John, but what was left of Newman's remains were moved as the Roman Catholic Church prepared to beatify him in 2010.
[56] There is, of course, disagreement within the progressive LGBT faith community as to whether same-sex marriage ultimately benefits queer people or is merely a way of reinscribing patriarchal values. See, e.g., Mary E. Hunt, "Same-Sex Marriage and Relational Justice," *Journal of Feminist Studies in Religion* 20, no. 2 (Fall 2004): 83–92.

Finally, with respect to the fourth source—experience—a queer theologian might turn to experiences of LGBT people in long-term relationships and examine how such relationships are in fact a visible manifestation of the invisible grace of God in the lives of such individuals. For example, Richard Hardy, a professor of spirituality and a gay man, has written about the lives of gay male couples who are touched by HIV/AIDS, and how the men in these relationships are "saints" who "live and love passionately, each in their own way, place, and time."[57]

As this example shows, "doing" queer theology is not simply a matter of advocacy or determining the "right" answer. Rather, it is an engagement with the four theological sources of scripture, tradition, reason, and experience, and reflecting deeply upon how LGBT people "talk about God."

Study Questions

1. How do you react to the definition of queer theology as "queer talk about God"?

2. How have you used the word "queer" in the past? How does it make you feel to use "queer" in the context of theology?

3. Describe each of the three definitions of "queer" as (a) an umbrella or collective term; (b) transgressive action; and (c) erasing boundaries. What are the three corresponding ways of understanding "queer theology"?

4. How does queer theory erase boundaries, particularly in the context of traditional categories of sexuality and gender identity? How does Christian theology also erase boundaries?

---

[57] Richard P. Hardy, *Loving Men: Gay Partners, Spirituality, and AIDS* (New York: Continuum, 1998), 183. For a discussion of how the sacred manifests itself in the sex lives of gay men, see David Nimmons, *The Soul Beneath the Skin: The Unseen Hearts and Habits of Gay Men* (New York: St. Martin's Griffin, 2002). For a general discussion of same-sex relationships and blessings, see Mark D. Jordan, ed., *Authorizing Marriage?: Canon, Tradition, and Critique in the Blessing of Same-Sex Unions* (Princeton, NJ: Princeton University Press, 2006).

5. Which of the four sources of queer theology—scripture, tradition, reason, and experience—appeals to you the most? The least?

6. Which of the various theological sources mentioned in support of same-sex marriage do you find the most persuasive?

For Further Study

Queer Theory
- Buchanan, *Oxford Dictionary of Critical Theory*, 393–94 ("queer studies," "queer theory").
- Edgar and Sedgwick, *Cultural Theory*, 277–78 ("queer theory").
- Hall, *Queer Theories*.
- Jagose, *Queer Theory*.
- Macey, *Dictionary of Critical Theory*, 321–22 ("queer").
- Stryker, *Transgender History*.
- Sullivan, *Critical Introduction to Queer Theory*.
- Turner, *Genealogy of Queer Theory*.
- Wilchins, *Queer Theory, Gender Theory*.

Defining Queer Theology
- Goss, *Queering Christ*, 223–58.
- Heyward, "We're Here, We're Queer."
- Loughlin, "Introduction."
- Shore-Goss, "Gay and Lesbian Theologies."
- Siker, "Queer Theology."
- Spencer, "Lesbian and Gay Theologies."
- Stuart, *Gay and Lesbian Theologies*.
- Stuart, *Religion Is a Queer Thing*.

Four Sources of Queer Theology

Scripture
- Drinkwater et al., *Torah Queeries*.
- Glaser, *The Word Is Out*.
- Goss, *Queering Christ*, 185–220 ("Homosexuality, the Bible, and the Practice of Safe Texts"; "Overthrowing Heterotextuality—A Biblical Stonewall").
- Goss and West, *Take Back the Word*.
- Guest, *When Deborah Met Jael*.
- Guest et al., *Queer Bible Commentary*.
- Hanks, *Subversive Gospel*.
- Helminiak, *What the Bible Really Says About Homosexuality*.
- Stone, *Queer Commentary and the Hebrew Bible*.
- Tanis, *Trans-Gendered*, 55–84 ("Gender Variance and the Scriptures").

Tradition
- Boswell, *Christianity, Social Tolerance, and Homosexuality*.
- Boswell, *Same-Sex Unions in Premodern Europe*.
- Brooten, *Love Between Women*.
- Brown, *Immodest Acts*.
- Burrus, *Sex Lives of Saints*.
- Jordan, *Invention of Sodomy in Christian Theology*.

Reason
- Armour and St. Ville, *Bodily Citations*.
- Bagemihl, *Biological Exuberance*.
- Bernauer and Carrette, *Michel Foucault and Theology*.
- Carrette, *Foucault and Religion*.
- Foucault, *Religion and Culture*.
- Moore, *Question of Truth*.

Experience
- Cannon, *Sanctified*.
- Evans and Healey, *Queer and Catholic*.
- Lake, *Recreations*.
- Sweasey, *From Queer to Eternity*.

Chapter Two

A Genealogy
of Queer Theology

How did queer theology come into being? Although the term "queer theology" is fairly new, LGBT-positive theological works actually have been in existence since the mid-1950s. This chapter will review the evolution of queer theology over the last half-century. Note that the term "queer" is being used here in a broad sense; that is, it is being used as an umbrella term to describe theology by and for LGBT people.

In particular, this chapter will review four different strands in the evolution of queer theology: (1) apologetic theology, (2) liberation theology, (3) relational theology, and (4) queer theology. The first strand, apologetic theology, can be summarized by the phrase "gay is good." Its primary purpose is to show that one can be both LGBT and Christian. The second strand, liberation theology, goes beyond mere acceptance and argues that liberation from the oppressions of heterosexism and homophobia is at the very heart of the gospel. The third strand, relational theology, centers upon the notion that God is found in the "erotic"—that is, in the midst of mutual relationship with another. The fourth and final strand, queer theology, challenges the notion that binary categories with respect to sexuality (for example, homosexuality vs. heterosexuality) or gender identity (for example, female vs. male) are fixed and impermeable.

It is important to note that these four strands of queer theology are not intended to divide the history of queer theology into distinct theological "eras." Rather, they are roughly chronological ways of describing certain trends in the development of queer theology over the last fifty years. Furthermore, these four strands are not mutually exclusive. That is, any given work of queer theology may contain one or more of these strands. For example, certain books relating to transgender theology might be considered queer theology because they challenge essentialist and binary conceptions of gender. However, such books might also be considered apologetic theology to the extent that they are arguing that "trans is good" and that one can be both a transgender person and a faithful Christian.

Four Strands of Queer Theology

Apologetic Theology

The first strand in the evolution of queer theology is apologetic theology. As noted above, this strand can be summarized by the slogan "gay is good." That is, these early theologians were primarily concerned with showing how LGBT (or, more accurately, gay and lesbian) people can be faithful Christians without the need to hide or change their sexuality, and how the Christian church should accept gays and lesbians as full members.

The first major work to rethink the traditionally negative relationship between Christianity and homosexuality was Derrick Sherwin Bailey's *Homosexuality and the Western Christian Tradition*, published in 1955 in the United Kingdom. Bailey, an Anglican priest, wrote the book because he wanted to "state as accurately and to examine as fully as possible" biblical and church attitudes toward homosexuality from the early church to the Middle Ages. Bailey concluded that the Western Christian tradition about homosexuality was both "erroneous" and "defective" because it had disregarded what Bailey called the "biological, psychological, or genetical" condition of "inversion," which was a term used to describe people who had a gay sexual orientation. That is, Bailey argued that the condition of inversion is an "inherent" and "apparently unalterable" condition that is itself "morally neutral." Because the invert is "impelled by his condition" to engage in same-sex acts, these acts should no longer be viewed as "acts of perversion." As such, Bailey believed that the Western Christian tradition "can no longer be regarded as an adequate guide by the theologian, the legislator, the sociologist, and the magistrate."[1]

---

[1] Bailey, *Homosexuality and the Western Christian Tradition*, vii, 168, 172–73.

Although it may seem surprising that a work such as Bailey's was published as early as 1955, there have been lesbian and gay church communities in existence since the 1940s. For example, the LGBT church historian Heather White has documented the founding of the Eucharistic Catholic Church in 1946 in Atlanta by a group of Catholics who had been denied the Eucharist because they had self-identified as homosexual. The group was led by a former Catholic seminarian who had been dismissed from seminary for having sex with another man. The group advertised as early in 1954 in *ONE Magazine*, a publication of the nascent "homophile" movement.[2]

In 1960, the openly gay Congregationalist minister Robert W. Wood published *Christ and the Homosexual (Some Observations)*, which was a groundbreaking work of gay theology. Wood suggested that the church should be true to its "message of love" by initiating "positive acts of concern" for the homosexual. Some of these positive acts would include encouraging the "homosexual" to "participate in Church activities." Wood also urged the church to "rethink[] the theological position on homosexuality" and the conditions under which same-sex acts might be moral. Wood concludes that homosexuality can in fact be moral if it "permits full expression" of one's personality and allows oneself to bring forth all of one's "redemptive love, mature adjustment and creativeness."[3]

Following the publication of Wood's book, a number of significant events occurred in the 1960s with respect to LGBT people and Christianity. In June 1964, the Council on Religion and the Homosexual (CRH) was established in San Francisco. The CRH was formed by a coalition of Protestant ministers and leaders from the gay community, and it recognized the need for dialogue between gay activists and communities of faith. In 1966, the national board of the YMCA published a book by H. Kimball Jones called *Toward a Christian Understanding of the Homosexual*, which challenged the "prejudices which have marred the vision of Christians through the ages" by presenting

---

[2] Heather Rachelle White, "Proclaiming Liberation: The Historical Roots of LGBT Religious Organizing, 1946–1976," *Nova Religio* 11, no. 4 (2008): 103–4.
[3] Robert W. Wood, *Christ and the Homosexual (Some Observations)* (New York: Vantage Press, 1960), 119, 207.

an "unbiased understanding" of homosexuality.[4] In 1967, the prominent Anglican process theologian Norman Pittenger published a 64-page booklet through the SCM Press called *Time for Consent?: A Christian's Approach to Homosexuality*— expanded to a book with the same title nearly a decade later— in which he presented a sustained argument as to why the church should "alter its attitude to homosexuals."[5]

In October 1968, the Reverend Troy Perry, a Pentecostal minister who had been expelled from his denomination for being gay, founded the Universal Fellowship of Metropolitan Community Churches (MCC) with twelve other people in his living room in Southern California. A few weeks before, Perry had placed an ad in *The Advocate*, a gay magazine. MCC has since grown into a worldwide denomination ministering to LGBT people and their allies in over thirty countries around the world. Perry later wrote about his journey as both a minister and a gay man in his 1972 autobiography, *The Lord Is My Shepherd and He Knows I'm Gay*.[6]

In the 1970s, a number of key works of apologetic theology were published. In 1976, John J. McNeill, a Jesuit priest, published *The Church and the Homosexual*, which had the stated purpose of reassessing the "traditional moral theology on the question of homosexuality within the Roman Catholic community."[7] McNeill had published a number of articles on homosexuality and Catholicism going back as far as 1970, but this book led to his silencing by the Vatican and his ultimate dismissal from the Jesuits.

In 1978, Letha Dawson Scanzoni and Virginia Ramey Mollenkott published *Is the Homosexual My Neighbor?: A Positive Christian Response*. Scanzoni and Mollenkott discussed the historical, biblical, scientific, and ethical bases for accepting gays and lesbians in the church, and they challenged Christians to accept homosexuals as their neighbors, just as Jesus had accepted the Samaritans, who also were outcasts in their day.[8]

[4] H. Kimball Jones, *Toward a Christian Understanding of the Homosexual* (New York: Association Press, 1966), 11.
[5] Norman Pittenger, *Time for Consent: A Christian's Approach to Homosexuality* (London: SCM Press, 1976), vii.
[6] See Troy Perry, *The Lord Is My Shepherd and He Knows I'm Gay* (Los Angeles: Nash Publishing, 1972).
[7] John J. McNeill, *The Church and the Homosexual*, 4th ed. (Boston: Beacon Press, 1993), 1.
[8] See Letha Dawson Scanzoni and Virginia Ramey Mollenkott, *Is the Homosexual My Neighbor?: A Positive Christian Response*, rev. and updated ed. (San Francisco: HarperSanFrancisco, 1994).

Apologetic theology reached its height with the publication in 1980 of John Boswell's *Christianity, Social Tolerance,
and Homosexuality*. In that book, Boswell argued that the early
church was not as uniformly homophobic as the tradition
would have us believe. According to Boswell, it was not until
the thirteenth century that the Christian church started to treat
same-sex acts with hostility and intolerance.[9] Although Boswell
was an academic historian, his work had an apologetic dimension in that he wanted the church to accept gay people for who
they are, and, conversely, for gay people to recognize that they
can be both Christian *and* gay.

Liberation Theology

The second strand in the evolution of queer theology is
liberation theology. This strand is modeled after the various
liberation theologies that came into being in the late 1960s
(for example, Latin American liberation theology and black
liberation theology), which were based upon the Exodus narrative of the Israelites being freed from their slavery in Egypt.
The primary concern of this strand was not just acceptance
of queer people by the church, but also the demonstration of
how queer liberation—that is, freedom from heterosexism and
homophobia, as well as the freedom to be one's own authentic
self—is at the very heart of the gospel message and Christian
theology.

Like the liberation theologies of Gustavo Gutiérrez and
James Cone,[10] the liberation strand of queer theology argued
that God was not neutral and in fact had a preferential option
for the poor and oppressed. For example, in 1968, the Anglican
priest H.W. Montefiore published a controversial essay, "Jesus,
the Revelation of God," which suggested that Jesus' celibacy might have been due to his being a homosexual. If so,
Montefiore argued, this would be "evidence of God's self-iden-
tification with those who are unacceptable to the upholders of
'The Establishment' and social conventions." That is, just as

---

[9] See Boswell, *Christianity, Social Tolerance, and Homosexuality*, 301–2.
[10] See, e.g., Gustavo Gutiérrez, *A Theology of Liberation: History, Politics, Salvation* (Maryknoll, NY: Orbis Books, 1973); James H. Cone, *Black Theology and Black Power* (New York: Harper and Row, 1969); James H. Cone, *A Black Theology of Liberation* (New York: J.B. Lippincott, 1970); James H. Cone, *God of the Oppressed* (New York: Seabury Press, 1975).

liberation theologians had argued in other contexts, Montefiore argued that God's nature was "befriending the friendless" and "identifying himself [sic] with the underprivileged."[11]

This focus on liberation theology appeared in other publications as well. For example, the September 1972 issue of *The Gay Christian*, a newsletter of the Metropolitan Community Church of New York, featured a number of articles about "gay theology." Howard Wells, the pastor of MCC New York at the time, wrote a provocative piece called "Gay God, Gay Theology" in which he described how the gay community has the right to refer to God—whom he called "our liberator, our redeemer"—as our "gay God." Wells rejected the notion of a God who would oppress gay people. Specifically, Wells said that any God who does so and "is blind to the enslavement of gay people" is nothing more than an "oppressive idol."[12]

In 1974, Sally Gearhart and William R. Johnson edited an anthology called *Loving Women/Loving Men: Gay Liberation and the Church*. In that volume, Johnson wrote an essay called "The Good News of Gay Liberation," in which he argued for the liberation of lesbians and gay men in the church. He noted that the "passive acceptance of injustice is no longer possible" for lesbian and gay people, and that the cry of "No more!" is especially applicable to the Christian church. Johnson proposed a number of goals for the church toward liberation, including the affirmation of same-sex relationships, electing gay people into church leadership positions, encouraging gay people to enroll in seminaries, and developing a "totally new theology of sexuality which would reflect the validity of same-sex relationships as well as other relationships and life styles."[13]

These early works of liberation theology were followed by a number of works in the late 1970s and 1980s with an unapologetically liberative bent. These works included *Towards a Theology of Gay Liberation*, a collection of essays published in

[11] H.W. Montefiore, "Jesus, the Revelation of God," in *Christ for Us Today*, ed. Norman Pittenger (London: SCM Press Ltd., 1968), 110.
[12] Howard R. Wells, "Gay God, Gay Theology," *The Gay Christian: Journal of the New York Metropolitan Community Church* 1, no. 5 (September 1972): 7–8.
[13] Bill Johnson, "The Good News of Gay Liberation," in *Loving Women / Loving Men: Gay Liberation and the Church*, ed. Sally Gearhart and William R. Johnson (San Francisco: Glide Publications, 1974), 91–92, 115–16.

1977 and edited by Malcolm Macourt, which included an essay about the relationship between Christian liberation and gay liberation and how the two "must impinge upon one another for better or for worse" because both deal with society as a whole.[14] Another work of gay liberation theology during this period was *Gay/Lesbian Liberation: A Biblical Perspective*, written by George R. Edwards and published in 1984, which argued for a biblically based theology of liberation for gays and lesbians.[15] In 1989, J. Michael Clark, a gay theologian, published *A Place to Start: Toward an Unapologetic Gay Liberation Theology*, in which he argued for "(re)constructing a gay liberation theology" that would rethink methodological issues as well as the importance of experience as a source for theology.[16]

The gay liberation strand of theology continued into the 1990s. In 1992, Robert Williams published *Just As I Am: A Practical Guide to Being Out, Proud, and Christian*. In that book, Williams contended that, consistent with the teachings of "Liberation Theology 101," only lesbians and gays can determine for themselves what constitutes sin and morality. For Williams, "*any* straight cleric's" attempt to define sin for gays and lesbians is "patriarchal and condescending" and ultimately "blasphemy."[17]

Similarly, in 1995 Richard Cleaver wrote *Know My Name: A Gay Liberation Theology*, in which he noted that the Latin American model of liberation theology demanded that lesbians and gay men—and not "religious experts"—work out a theology of "homosexuality" for themselves.[18] In sum, what all of these works shared in common, from the 1960s through the 1990s, was the assertion that the gospel and the Christian faith demands that queer people be liberated from the bondage of heterosexism and homophobia.

---

[14] Giles Hibbert, "Gay Liberation in Relation to Christian Liberation," in *Towards a Theology of Gay Liberation*, ed. Malcolm Macourt (London: SCM Press, 1977), 91.

[15] See George R. Edwards, *Gay/Lesbian Liberation: A Biblical Perspective* (New York: Pilgrim Press, 1984).

[16] J. Michael Clark, *A Place to Start: Toward an Unapologetic Gay Liberation Theology* (Dallas, TX: Monument Press, 1989), 27.

[17] Williams, *Just As I Am*, 151–52.

[18] Richard Cleaver, *Know My Name: A Gay Liberation Theology* (Louisville, KY: Westminster John Knox Press, 1995), 12.

Relational Theology

The third strand in the evolution of queer theology is relational theology. This strand was developed primarily by lesbian theologians as a response to the silence in gay male theology about women's issues and the importance of feminist theological reflection. This strand of queer theology focused not so much on issues of acceptance or liberation, but rather finding God in the midst of the erotic—that is, mutual relationship—with another person.

Lesbian theological voices first started to emerge in the late 1960s and early 1970s. In the beginning, these writings were primarily apologetic in nature. For example, in 1969 Barbara B. Gittings wrote an essay called "The Homosexual and the Church" in which she argued that it was the duty of the Christian church to welcome lesbians and gay men. She argued that the church should "make an affirmative, active effort to accept and welcome the homosexual, unreservedly and openly . . . and to equality in the worship of his [sic] God."[19] Interestingly, Gittings wrote only about the "homosexual" in generic terms and did not make a distinction between lesbians and gay men.

In 1971, Del Martin and Phyllis Lyon—the founders of the Daughters of Bilitis, which was the first social and political group for lesbians in the United States—wrote "A Lesbian Approach to Theology." In that essay, Martin and Lyon challenged various stereotypes about lesbians, including the stereotype of a "predatory, masculinized woman who spends all her time seducing young girls." Martin and Lyon, who also worked with the Council on Religion and the Homosexual in San Francisco, argued that the "despairing homosexual" must understand that "he [sic] too is a child of God."[20]

In 1974, Sally Gearhart wrote an essay, "The Miracle of Lesbianism," which was published in the *Loving Women/Loving Men* anthology. This essay was an important step toward the development of relational theology because it focused upon

---

[19] Barbara B Gittings, "The Homosexual and the Church," in *The Same Sex: An Appraisal of Homosexuality*, ed. Ralph W. Weltge (Philadelphia: Pilgrim Press, 1969), 155.

[20] Del Martin and Phyllis Lyon, "A Lesbian Approach to Theology," in *Is Gay Good?: Ethics, Theology, and Homosexuality*, ed. W. Dwight Oberholtzer (Philadelphia: Westminster Press, 1971), 216, 219.

the importance of *relationships* for lesbians. For Gearhart, the "cause" of lesbianism is nothing more than a self-love that "expresses itself in love of other women and thus in rebellion of a woman-hating society." Being a lesbian is a "mind-set, life-style, a body of experience" of being truly "woman-identified," whether or not that is expressed in terms of a physical relationship with another woman. As such, Gearhart argued that lesbians can be reunited with their heterosexual sisters through feminism.[21]

A significant turning point in relational theology occurred in 1989 with the publication of *Touching Our Strength: The Erotic as Power and the Love of God* by Carter Heyward. In that book, Heyward draws upon Audre Lorde's view of the erotic as sacred and argues that God is not extrinsic to sex or gender, but rather "is immersed in our gendered and erotic particularities." For Heyward, God exists in the connection that women have with "body and nature and darkness and moisture and dirt and sex."[22] What was distinctive about Heyward's work was that not only did it draw upon her embodied experiences as a lesbian, but it also was a different way of doing theology.

Following Heyward, a number of lesbian theologians have also focused on relationality in their theological works. This included Mary E. Hunt, the cofounder and codirector of Women's Alliance for Theology, Ethics, and Ritual (WATER), who in her 1991 book *Fierce Tenderness: A Feminist Theology of Friendship* articulated a theology of friendship in which she argues that human friendship (whether or not including "genital expression") is a "useful paradigm of right relation for the whole of creation."[23] Similarly, Elizabeth Stuart, a lesbian theologian at the University of Winchester, articulated an agenda for the broader Christian church in her 1995 book *Just Good Friends: Towards a Lesbian and Gay Theology of Relationships* that included the need to practice an ethic of friendship and to "sacramentalize" friendship.[24] Both Hunt and Stuart focused on

---

[21] Sally Gearhart, "The Miracle of Lesbianism," in Gearhart and Johnson, *Loving Women/Loving Men*, 128, 133.

[22] Heyward, *Touching Our Strength*, 103.

[23] Mary E. Hunt, *Fierce Tenderness: A Feminist Theology of Friendship* (New York: Crossroad, 1991), 2.

[24] Elizabeth Stuart, *Just Good Friends: Towards a Lesbian and Gay Theology of Relationships* (London: Mowbray, 1995), 236.

friendship as a central theme for constructing their respective relational theologies and where God is ultimately found.

Even gay male theologians and ethicists in the 1990s were influenced strongly by theologies of relationality. These included Gary David Comstock, the former Protestant chaplain at Wesleyan University, who in his 1993 book *Gay Theology Without Apology* argued that we should think of Jesus more as a friend and not a master.[25] These also included Daniel T. Spencer, a professor at the University of Montana, whose work in lesbian and gay ecological ethics in his 1996 book *Gay and Gaia: Ethics, Ecology, and the Erotic* was expressly grounded in the "erotic" and the "deep sense of interconnection" as articulated by relational theologians such as Carter Heyward.[26] Finally, this included scholars such as Marvin M. Ellison, a gay ethicist at Bangor Theological Seminary, who constructed an ethic of sexuality in his 1996 book *Erotic Justice: A Liberating Ethic of Sexuality* that affirmed the "godly power of loving body touch."[27]

Finally, much of the somber theological reflection by gay male theologians that arose in the 1980s out of the HIV/AIDS pandemic can be understood in relational terms. For example, John E. Fortunato in his 1987 book *AIDS, the Spiritual Dilemma* described the spiritual journey as a union with God. Fortunato proposed that the only way to deal with the anger and pain of unjust natural evils such as HIV/AIDS is, paradoxically, through "acts of loving—of tending the sick and dying, of comforting the bereaved, and of striving to find a cure."[28]

Queer Theology

The fourth strand in the evolution of queer theology is queer theology itself. This strand is based upon the theoretical work of queer theorists such as Michel Foucault, Judith Butler, and Eve Kosofsky Sedgwick. Specifically, queer theology challenges the essentialist notions of sexuality and gender identity, and it argues that these concepts are not so much "fixed" but

---

[25] See Gary David Comstock, *Gay Theology Without Apology* (Cleveland, OH: Pilgrim Press, 1993).

[26] See Daniel T. Spencer, *Gay and Gaia: Ethics, Ecology, and the Erotic* (Cleveland, OH: Pilgrim Press, 1996).

[27] Marvin M. Ellison, *Erotic Justice: A Liberating Ethic of Sexuality* (Louisville, KY: Westminster John Knox Press, 1996), 120.

[28] John E. Fortunato, *AIDS, the Spiritual Dilemma* (San Francisco: Harper and Row, 1987), 118.

rather socially constructed through language and discourse.[29] As noted above, a constructivist view of sexuality and gender identity doesn't deny the fact that there are individuals who are born with same-sex attractions and/or gender variant identities and who remain that way throughout their lives. It does mean, however, that the cultural meaning and significance of such sexual attractions and gender expressions are fluid depending upon a particular time and place.

By definition, these queer theologies include bisexual and transgender theologies because these discourses inherently deconstruct binary notions of sexuality (that is, bisexual discourse challenges the heterosexuality vs. homosexuality binary) and gender identity (that is, transgender discourse challenges the male vs. female binary) in favor of a more fluid understanding of sexuality and gender identity as points along a spectrum or continuum.

This challenging of essentialist notions of sexuality in a theological context can be traced at least as far back as 1973, to Mary Daly's *Beyond God the Father: Toward a Philosophy of Women's Liberation*. In that work, Daly rejects the "heterosexuality-homosexuality" dichotomy as "destructive" because these are still "patriarchal classifications" that reinforce the "sex role system." For Daly, the category of "homosexuality" is still "not radical enough" because the sex of one's partner ultimately still matters with respect to that category. Furthermore, according to Daly, the term "homosexual" is used as a "scare term" to "intimidate those who even appear to deviate from the norms dictated by role psychology" and, as such, is actually an "instrument of social control."[30]

One of the earliest discussions of queer theory in the specific context of LGBT theology occurred in 1993 with Robert E. Shore-Goss's *Jesus Acted Up: A Gay and Lesbian Manifesto*. Shore-Goss uses the term "queer" throughout the work and also refers to Foucault's work and the constructed nature of

---

[29] For an overview of the theoretical issues relating to queer theology, see Laurel C. Schneider, "Homosexuality, Queer Theory, and Christian Theology," in *Men and Masculinities in Christianity and Judaism: A Critical Reader*, ed. Björn Krondorfer (London: SCM Press, 2009), 63–76.

[30] Mary Daly, *Beyond God the Father: Toward a Philosophy of Women's Liberation* (Boston: Beacon Press, 1973), 24–27.

sexuality in an appendix.[31] Nevertheless, it is fair to say that Shore-Goss's overall work was still grounded in a liberationist conception of lesbian and gay identity. In 1997, Gary David Comstock and Susan E. Henking edited *Que(e)rying Religion: A Critical Anthology*, which expressly acknowledged the influence of queer studies upon the works in that anthology.[32] Also in 1997, Mark Jordan published *The Invention of Sodomy in Christian Theology* in which he builds upon queer theory to caution against an essentialist reading of gay and lesbian identity. Specifically, Jordan argues that when "we lesbians and gays think of ourselves as members of a tribe, as a separate people or race, we echo medieval theology's preoccupation with the Sodomites."[33]

Queer theology came of age in 2000 with the publication of Marcella Althaus-Reid's *Indecent Theology: Theological Perversions in Sex, Gender and Politics*. In that book, Althaus-Reid set forth a shocking "indecent theology"—including discussions of the scent of Latin American women who do not wear underwear, being in bed with the Madonna, engaging in french kissing with God, and doing theology in corset-laced leather boots—that unmasked the heterosexual and patriarchal assumptions of traditional liberation theologies.[34] In the same year, Laura Dykstra published an essay, "Jesus, Bread, Wine and Roses: A Bisexual Feminist at the Catholic Worker," which reflected upon her experiences as a Roman Catholic bisexual woman.[35]

Since *Indecent Theology*, there have been a number of works that have examined queer theology from a more systematic perspective. In 2002, Shore-Goss published *Queering Christ: Beyond Jesus Acted Up*, which contained a chapter, "Transgression as a Metaphor for Queer Theologies," which explored more fully the intersections of queer theory and theology.[36] In 2003, Elizabeth Stuart published *Gay and Lesbian*

---

[31] See Robert Goss, *Jesus Acted Up: A Gay and Lesbian Manifesto* (San Francisco: HarperSanFrancisco, 1993), 181–90.
[32] See Gary David Comstock and Susan E. Henking, eds., *Que(e)rying Religion: A Critical Anthology* (New York: Continuum, 1997).
[33] Jordan, *Invention of Sodomy in Christian Theology*, 163.
[34] See Althaus-Reid, *Indecent Theology*.
[35] See Dykstra, "Jesus, Bread, Wine and Roses," 78–88.
[36] Goss, *Queering Christ*, 223–38.

Theologies: Repetitions with Critical Difference, which was a chronological history of LGBT theology and discussed how her own views on queer theology have evolved over time.[37] In 2007, Gerard Loughlin published *Queer Theology: Rethinking the Western Body*, which was a provocative collection of essays on the intersections of queer theory and theology.[38]

Finally, there have been an increasing number of works on transgender theology in recent years. The earliest works, written in the 1990s, involved cross-dressing and transvestism. For example, Eleanor McLaughlin, an Episcopal priest, published an essay on christology and cross-dressing in 1993 called "Feminist Christologies: Re-Dressing the Tradition."[39] This was followed in 1996 by *Cross Purposes: On Being Christian and Crossgendered*, which was a monograph written by Vanessa Sheridan under the name of "Vanessa S."[40]

An important milestone with respect to transgender theology occurred in 2001 with the publication of Virginia Ramey Mollenkott's *Omnigender: A Trans-Religious Approach*, which was a comprehensive discussion of the problems with the bi-gender system in the context of Christianity and Judaism as well as other world religious traditions.[41] This was followed in 2003 with *Transgender Journeys*, coauthored by Sheridan and Mollenkott.[42] In the same year, Justin Tanis published *Trans-Gendered: Theology, Ministry and Communities of Faith*.[43] In 2004, Leanne McCall Tigert and Maren C. Tirabassi edited a volume of essays called *Transgendering Faith: Identity, Sexuality, and Spirituality*.[44] Most recently, Althaus-Reid and Lisa Isherwood, a feminist liberation theologian at the University of Winchester, edited an anthology on transgender theology called *Trans/Formations*, which was published in 2009.[45]

---

[37] See Stuart, *Gay and Lesbian Theologies*.
[38] See Loughlin, *Queer Theology*.
[39] See Eleanor McLaughlin, "Feminist Christologies: Re-Dressing the Tradition," in *Reconstructing the Christ Symbol: Essays in Feminist Christology*, ed. Maryanne Stevens (New York: Paulist Press, 1993), 118–49.
[40] See Vanessa S., *Cross Purposes: On Being Christian and Crossgendered* (Decatur, GA: Sullivan Press, 1996).
[41] See Virginia Ramey Mollenkott, *Omnigender: A Trans-Religious Approach* (Cleveland, OH: Pilgrim Press, 2001).
[42] See Virginia Ramey Mollenkott and Vanessa Sheridan, *Transgender Journeys* (Cleveland, OH: Pilgrim Press, 2003).
[43] See Justin Tanis, *Trans-Gendered: Theology, Ministry, and Communities of Faith* (Cleveland, OH: Pilgrim Press, 2003).
[44] See Leanne McCall Tigert and Maren C. Tirabassi, eds., *Transgendering Faith: Identity, Sexuality, and Spirituality* (Cleveland, OH: Pilgrim Press, 2004).
[45] See Althaus-Reid and Isherwood, *Trans/formations;* For a Jewish perspective, see Dmurza, *Balancing on the Mechitza*.

Future Trends: Intersectionality and Hybridity

Where is queer theology headed in the future? One noticeable trend is the increasing focus by queer theologians on issues of race, class, and other factors in addition to sexuality and gender identity. These issues are grounded in notions of intersectionality from critical race theory, as well as hybridity from postcolonial theology.[46] As in the case with queer theology, these works are less concerned with fixed identities and identity politics, but rather with the ways in which these identities are fluid and constantly changing, depending upon the power dynamics of a given social context.

Some queer theologians of color who have addressed issues of intersectionality and hybridity include Renée L. Hill, Elias Farajajé-Jones, and myself. Hill, a lesbian African American Episcopal priest, has written about developing a "multireligious, multidialogical" process that arises out of her own "multiply intersected life." For Hill, this means examining sources from other religions in the African Diaspora, including Islam, Santeria, Akan, Yoruba, Vodun, Buddhism, Judaism, and Humanism. She notes that black liberation theologies need to be "knocked off-center" by entering into a "multidialogical process."[47]

In addition to Hill, Elias Farajajé-Jones, a bisexual and biracial theologian at the Starr King School for Ministry, has written about the lethal intersections between homophobia, biphobia, AIDS-phobia, sexism, and heterosexism within the African American community. According to Farajajé-Jones, these oppressions arise out of a "Eurocentric interpretation of Christianity, which is rooted in an either/or view of the world" that is "quite literally killing us." He concludes that a truly prophetic black theology would join the struggle against "heteropatriarchy, the source of multitudinous forms of oppression."[48]

---

[46] For some recent theological works on hybridity, see Brian Bantum, *Redeeming Mulatto: A Theology of Race and Christian Hybridity* (Waco, TX: Baylor University Press, 2010); and Patrick S. Cheng, "Rethinking Sin and Grace for LGBT People Today," in Ellison and Douglas, *Sexuality and the Sacred*, 105–18.

[47] Renée Leslie Hill, "Disrupted/Disruptive Movements: Black Theology and Black Power 1969/1999," in *Black Faith and Public Talk: Critical Essays on James H. Cone's Black Theology and Black Power*, ed. Dwight N. Hopkins (Maryknoll, NY: Orbis Books, 1999), 147.

[48] Elias Farajajé-Jones, "Breaking Silence: Toward an In-the-Life Theology," in *Black Theology: A Documentary History, Volume II, 1980–1992*, ed. James H. Cone and Gayraud S. Wilmore (Maryknoll, NY: Orbis Books, 1993), 158.

Finally, much of my own theological reflection has related to my multiply intersected life as a queer Asian American theologian. For example, I have written about the experiences of LGBT Asian Americans due to multiple naming, multiple silencing, multiple oppression, and multiple fragmentation.[49] Like Hill, I cite the importance of reclaiming other religious traditions—for example, Buddhism, Confucianism, Daoism, and Hinduism—as well as other rites, rituals, and sacred spaces.[50]

As Robert Shore-Goss has written, one danger of queer theology is a "gay theological hegemony" that excludes other voices in "various shades of contextualities." In other words, Shore-Goss encourages LGBT theologians to be in dialogue with the diverse contextual and liberation theologies that have emerged since the 1960s, including Latin American, black, womanist, Latina/o, Asian, Asian American, Native American, disability and other theologies. Shore-Goss has encouraged the development of new "shades, variants, and tonalities" in queer theologies, and that is precisely what many queer theologians of color are seeking to do.[51]

---

[49] See Patrick S. Cheng, "Multiplicity and Judges 19: Constructing a Queer Asian Pacific American Biblical Hermeneutic," *Semeia* 90/91 (2002): 119–33.

[50] See Patrick S. Cheng, "Reclaiming Our Traditions, Rituals, and Spaces: Spirituality and the Queer Asian Pacific American Experience," *Spiritus* 6, no. 2 (Fall 2006): 234–40.

[51] Goss, *Queering Christ*, 253.

Study Questions

1. What are the four strands in the evolution of queer theology? Are these categories mutually exclusive or not?

2. How would you characterize the main purpose of apologetic theology? Liberation theology? Relational theology? Queer theology?

3. Which strand of queer theology speaks the most strongly to you? Which strand is the least appealing to you? Why?

4. Have you ever used apologetic arguments to defend a theological position or doctrine?

5. What is the importance of liberation to you and your community? How is the Christian gospel consistent with liberation?

6. How does the relational strand of queer theology help to ensure that women's (and, in particular, lesbians') voices are heard?

7. What do you think about the emergence of bisexual and transgender theologies? How do such theologies challenge sexual and gender binaries?

8. What are some future trends of queer theology, particularly with respect to intersectionality and hybridity?

For Further Study

Historical Overview
- Goss, *Queering Christ*, 239–58 ("From Gay Theology to Queer Sexual Theologies").
- Shore-Goss, "Gay and Lesbian Theologies."
- Siker, "Queer Theology."
- Spencer, "Lesbian and Gay Theologies."
- Stuart, *Gay and Lesbian Theologies.*

Apologetic Theology
- Bailey, *Homosexuality and the Western Christian Tradition.*
- Boswell, *Christianity, Social Tolerance, and Homosexuality.*
- McNeill, *Church and the Homosexual.*
- Scanzoni and Mollenkott, *Is the Homosexual My Neighbor?*
- Wood, *Christ and the Homosexual.*

Liberation Theology
- Clark, *A Place to Start.*
- Edwards, *Gay/Lesbian Liberation.*
- Gearhart and Johnson, *Loving Women/ Loving Men.*
- Macourt, *Towards a Theology of Gay Liberation.*
- Williams, *Just as I Am.*

Relational Theology
- Comstock, *Gay Theology Without Apology*
- Gearhart, "The Miracle of Lesbianism."
- Heyward, *Touching Our Strength.*
- Hunt, *Fierce Tenderness.*
- Spencer, *Gay and Gaia.*
- Stuart, *Just Good Friends.*

Queer Theology
- Althaus-Reid, *Indecent Theology.*
- Althaus-Reid and Isherwood, *Trans/ formations.*
- Goss, *Queering Christ.*
- Jordan, *Invention of Sodomy in Christian Theology.*
- Loughlin, *Queer Theology.*
- Mollenkott, *Omnigender.*
- Schneider, "Homosexuality, Queer Theory, and Christian Theology."
- Tanis, *Trans-Gendered.*

Future Trends
- Cheng, "Reclaiming Our Traditions, Rituals, and Spaces."
- Cheng, "Rethinking Sin and Grace for LGBT People Today."
- Farajajé-Jones, "Breaking Silence."
- Hill, "Disrupted/Disruptive Movements."

Chapter Three

God: The Sending Forth of Radical Love

Having explored the definitions, sources, and genealogy of queer theology, we now turn to the substantive doctrines of queer theology. As noted earlier, this book will follow the general three-part structure of the Apostles' Creed and Nicene Creed. The first section of each of these creeds relates to the doctrine of God, who is the first person of the Trinity and the creator of all that is seen and unseen.

The main theme of this chapter is that God is the *sending forth of radical love*. As we have seen earlier, radical love is defined as a love that is so extreme that it dissolves existing boundaries. Not only is God love,[1] but God is a love that is described in terms of extreme wealth and superabundance.[2] In other words, not only is God defined as radical love itself, but God's very being consists of the continuous sending forth of this radical love to others.

In this chapter, we will examine four classical theological doctrines about God. The first doctrine is *revelation*, or how human beings can come to know a God who is transcendent and beyond our comprehension. The second doctrine is that of *God*, or the first person of the Trinity. The third doctrine is that of the *Trinity*, by which we understand God as both three and one. The fourth doctrine is that of *creation*, or the relationship between God and the created order. We will examine what queer theologians have written about these doctrines and also how they relate to radical love.

Revelation: God's Coming Out as Radical Love

How do we know about God? How is it possible for us, as humans, to know who God is and what God's relationship to us

---

[1] 1 John 4:8.
[2] Eph. 1:18 (*ploutos*); Rom. 5:20 (*huperperisseuō*).

is all about? These are the questions addressed by the doctrine of revelation. Traditionally speaking, God reveals Godself to humanity in at least two ways: first, through scripture and, second, through human reason. Take, for example, the proposition that God is the creator of the universe. First, this proposition is revealed to us in scripture through the first chapter of Genesis in the Bible.[3] Second, this proposition is revealed to us through reason because we can observe that every effect has a cause and that, working backward, there must be a very first cause, which is what we call God.

From the perspective of queer theology, however, the doctrine of revelation is more than just a matter of scripture or reason. It is also a matter of experience. Specifically, the doctrine of revelation can be understood as *God's coming out as radical love*. In other words, the doctrine of revelation parallels the self-disclosure that occurs when an LGBT person comes out to someone whom she or he loves about her or his sexuality and/or gender identity. God reveals Godself to us because God loves us and wants to share Godself with us. From scripture, we know that God is love,[4] that God so loved the world that God became incarnate so that we could share in God's eternal life,[5] and that the greatest commandments are to love God with all of one's heart, soul, and mind, and to love one's neighbor as oneself.[6] Ultimately, God's coming out is an act of radical love because, like the coming out experience for LGBT people, it results in the dissolving of existing boundaries.

Dissolving Boundaries between the Divine and Human

First, God's revelation—or coming out—is an act of radical love because it dissolves the boundaries between the divine and human. That is, God reaches out to us by breaking through the divide between the divine and human. Otherwise, we would have no way to speak about, let alone comprehend, God. It is precisely through the doctrine of revelation that the seemingly infinite gap between the divine and the human can

---

[3] Gen. 1:1.
[4] 1 John 4:8.
[5] John 3:16.
[6] Mark 12:29–31; Matt. 22:37–38.

be bridged. Indeed, without revelation, God would remain an abstract mystery to us—that is, "out there" as opposed to being Emmanuel, or "God-with-us," right here. This revelation, particularly when it occurs in the form of scripture, can be understood as a love letter—or e-mail, chat, text message, tweet, or Facebook post—from God to us![7]

Similarly, whenever an LGBT person comes out to another person about her or his sexuality or gender identity, the previously existing boundary between the LGBT person and the other person is dissolved. In other words, the divide between the LGBT person's "public" and "private" lives is erased. Coming out, as an act of boundary crossing, challenges society's traditional view that issues of sexuality and gender identity should remain unspoken and outside the realm of public discourse. Coming out, therefore, is an act of radical love that parallels how God reveals Godself to us through revelation.

Dissolving Boundaries between the Powerful and Weak

Second, God's revelation—or coming out—is an act of radical love because it dissolves the boundaries between the powerful and weak. For example, Chris Glaser, an openly gay theologian and minister with the Metropolitan Community Churches, has written about how God's revelation as Jesus Christ disrupts the traditional divide between the powerful and the weak. Glaser notes that the "story of the New Testament is that God comes out of the closet of heaven and out of the religious system of the time to reveal Godself in the person of Jesus Christ."[8] For example, God's coming out as the infant Jesus in the incarnation reveals God's solidarity with the marginalized and vulnerable, and not just the powerful and the elite. Similarly, God's coming out as the Jesus who ministers to those who are "unclean" reveals God's preferential option for the outcast and the excluded, and not just religiously "respectable" people. Indeed, God "chose what is weak in the world to shame the strong."[9]

---

[7] For example, Mark Jordan has described the epistle form of writing in "less churchy language" as a "love letter." See Mark D. Jordan, *Telling Truths in Church: Scandal, Flesh, and Christian Speech* (Boston: Beacon Press, 2003), 107.

[8] Chris Glaser, *Coming Out as Sacrament* (Louisville, KY: Westminster John Knox Press, 1998), 85.

[9] 1 Cor. 1:27.

Olive Hinnant, an openly lesbian minister with the United Church of Christ, explores how the boundaries between LGBT people (here, the weak) and the church (here, the powerful) are dissolved through God's revelation in the preached Word. Specifically, Hinnant argues that God "comes out of heterosexism" whenever an openly LGBT clergyperson preaches the Word. That is, the "closet door opens" and reveals a "gay God who longs to be welcomed into full communion."[10] In the same way that Jesus is the embodied revelation of the ineffable "God," coming out allows the LGBT minister to become an embodied revelation of the abstract notion of "homosexuality" or "queerness." In this way, the boundaries between LGBT people and the church are dissolved.

Dissolving Boundaries between Knowing and Unknowing

Third, God's revelation—or coming out—is an act of radical love because it dissolves the boundaries between knowing and unknowing. According to the mystical tradition of apophatic or negative theology, God can never be fully known in a positive sense. Because God is beyond all of our limited human senses, God can only be known through an ongoing process of unknowing. Susannah Cornwall, a queer theologian and research fellow at the University of Exeter, has written about the connection between *apophasis*, revelation, and the transgender experience in her essay "Apophasis and Ambiguity." According to Cornwall, to the extent that the category of "transgender" resists the binary opposition of "heterosexual" and "homosexual," it can be understood as a form of *apophasis*.

For Cornwall, the transgender experience—like the mystical experience of God—is a state of apophatic "unknowing." It is a state of resisting any final "knowledge" of the polarities of "heterosexual" and "homosexual." Indeed, it is a state of being in perpetual transformation, just as Gregory of Nyssa described the human journey toward the divine as *epektasis*, or "never arriving at any limit of perfection." For Cornwall, there can never be a sense of "arrival." Both divine revelation

---

[10] Olive Elaine Hinnant, *God Comes Out: A Queer Homiletic* (Cleveland, OH: Pilgrim Press, 2007), 168.

and the transgender experience reject a "climactic picture of perfection in favour of a transformative one based on uncertainty and continual journeying." This "living in tension" and "often discomfiting uncertainty" is what it means to grow as a human being.[11]

To summarize, the doctrine of revelation can be understood as God coming out to us. This self-revelation is grounded in God's love for us, and it is a radical kind of love because it dissolves existing boundaries that separate the divine from the human, the powerful from the weak, and knowing from unknowing. In fact, the doctrine of revelation can be understood in terms of apophatic (or negative) theology, in which our knowledge of God—like our understanding of the category of "transgender"—is always in a state of transformation and unknowing.

[11] Susannah Cornwall, "Apophasis and Ambiguity: The 'Unknowingness' of Transgender," in Althaus-Reid and Isherwood, *Trans/formations*, 25. For the tension between the kataphatic and apophatic ways of knowing in a queer theological context, see Michael Bernard Kelly, "A Potential for Transformation: Gay Men and the Future of Christian Spirituality," in *Sources of Transformation: Revitalising Christian Spirituality*, ed. Edward Howells and Peter Tyler (London: Continuum, 2010).

Study Questions

1. How can revelation be understood as God's coming out?

2. Have you or someone you know come out of the closet? What is the role of love in the decision to come out?

3. How does God reveal Godself to you? Through scripture, tradition, reason, and/or experience?

4. How does the doctrine of revelation dissolve the boundaries between the divine and the human? The powerful and the weak? Knowing and unknowing?

5. What are some connections between the doctrine of revelation and the transgender experience?

For Further Study

Revelation
- Cornwall, "Apophasis and Ambiguity."
- Glaser, *Coming Out as Sacrament*, 77–95 ("God Comes Out").
- Hinnant, *God Comes Out*.
- Kelly, "A Potential for Transformation."

God: Radical Love Itself

What do we mean when we talk about God? Who is God for LGBT people? Many people think of God as the bearded old man on the ceiling of the Sistine Chapel who creates and rules over the universe. Indeed, this image recalls the traditional way of describing the first person of the Trinity as "God the Father." These paternal images of God are imperfect descriptions, however, because a truly transcendent God is ultimately beyond human categories, including sex and gender. We can only talk about God through analogical language.

God—like queer relationships—can be understood as *radical love itself*. In other words, God is the very manifestation of a love that is so extreme that it dissolves existing boundaries, including the traditional divide between the divine and the human. This "bridging of the gap" is especially true in the incarnation, in which God becomes human in the person of Jesus Christ. In the same way, LGBT relationships are grounded in a love so extreme that it also dissolves existing boundaries between the self and the other, as well as rigid societal boundaries as to gender roles (for example, traditionally speaking, a man can be married only to a woman, and not to another man).

God as Radical Love

What does it mean in practical terms to say that God is radical love itself? The Bible is clear that God is love.[12] In fact, it can be argued that the main theme of the Bible is love, whether it is manifested through God's *hesed* (that is, steadfast love) in the Hebrew Bible, or in Jesus proclaiming that the greatest commandments are to love God and one's neighbor as oneself,[13] as well as giving his disciples a new commandment to love one another as he has loved them.[14]

But this love is not just any love, but a radical kind of love. It is a love so extreme that it dissolves existing boundaries that might normally seem fixed. We know that God's love is extreme in terms of magnitude because God's grace is described in

---

[12] 1 John 4:8.
[13] Mark 12:29–31; Matt. 22:37–38.
[14] John 15:12.

superlative terms.[15] However, God's love is also extreme because it breaks down all kinds of human boundaries—not just the boundary between the divine and the human as discussed earlier in the context of the doctrine of revelation, but also the boundary between life and death (as seen in the death and resurrection of Jesus Christ).

As such, God functions in the same way as LGBT people with respect to radical love. To the extent that LGBT people break down boundaries of sexuality and gender in our relationships, both God and LGBT people send forth a radical love that breaks down fixed categories and boundaries. For God, these categories include the divine and human, and life and death. For LGBT people, these boundaries include the categories of female and male, and homosexual and heterosexual.

Carter Heyward has argued that God is found in the erotic—that is, the "shared experience of relational power"—between not just human beings, but also with other creatures and nature.[16] Thus, God has a "fluid sense of gender" that is manifested in "erotic friendship" among all creatures in creation.[17] Heyward's view of God as pure relationality has been highly influential and even can be seen in the work of gay male theologians such as Gary Comstock, who has argued that God is not so much "above, other, or outside" of us, but rather "among, between, and part of us."[18]

Parodying God as Divine "Top"

Another way in which the doctrine of God can be viewed as radical love—that is, a love so extreme that it dissolves categories—is through parody. As Elizabeth Stuart has noted, parody is not just a "simple sending up" of the thing to be parodied. Rather, it is an "extended repetition with critical difference." In other words, parody can be seen as "improvising on a theme, non-identical repetition," and this theme becomes "freshly embodied in different contexts."[19]

---

[15] Eph. 1:18 (*ploutos*); Rom. 5:20 (*huperperisseuō*).
[16] Heyward, *Touching Our Strength*, 99.
[17] Heyward, *Touching Our Strength*, 103.
[18] Comstock, *Gay Theology Without Apology*, 129.
[19] Stuart, *Gay and Lesbian Theologies*, 108.

For example, the Christian Eucharist is a parody to the extent that it is a repetition of the Jewish seder meal, but with a "critical difference" of the "inauguration of a new covenant."[20] Drag is a parody in that it is a performance of a gendered role, but with the "critical difference" of disrupting societal norms about gender identities. These parodies dissolve categories because they attempt to replicate the thing to be parodied, but the copy is ultimately transformed into a new creation.

Queer theologians have parodied God's traditional divine attribute of omnipotence—that is, God's all-powerful nature—by superimposing sexual roles on God. For example, Theodore Jennings, a theologian at Chicago Theological Seminary, has suggested that YHWH, the God of the Hebrew Bible, can be understood as being the "top" in a homoerotic relationship with David, the king of Israel—akin to that of a warrior chief and his boy companion. For Jennings, YHWH's relationship with David is actually a representation of YHWH's relationship to Israel, and thus it creates an erotic relationship between the divine and the human. As such, this relationship can be described in terms of "top" (YHWH) and "bottom" (Israel) in terms of the same warrior chief and boy companion dynamic described above.[21] Similarly, Gerard Loughlin has written about God's phallus, which is "often imitated, but never seen" and yet "deflowers" each Israelite male through the act of circumcision.[22]

Roland Boer, a theologian and research professor at the University of Newcastle, also imagines YHWH as a sexual "top" with respect to humans. In particular, Boer argues that YHWH engages in a sadomasochistic relationship with humans. Indeed, according to Boer, all of the "basic features of masochism" appear in the Bible: "fetishes, fantasy, imagination, covenant, law, beating, whipping, binding, construction of the torturer, atmosphere, suspension, waiting, and even the oral mother."[23] Here, Boer superimposes the leather culture of

---

[20] Stuart, *Gay and Lesbian Theologies*, 108.
[21] See Theodore W. Jennings, "YHWH as Erastes," in Stone, *Queer Commentary and the Hebrew Bible*, 36–74.
[22] Gerard Loughlin, "Omphalos," in Loughlin, *Queer Theology*, 125.
[23] Roland Boer, "Yahweh as Top: A Lost Targum," in Stone, *Queer Commentary and the Hebrew Bible*, 105.

bondage and discipline, domination and submission, and sado-masochism (BDSM) on God. As Thomas Peterson has noted in his provocative essay "Gay Men's Spiritual Experience in the Leather Community," leathersex can be a highly spiritual experience, although usually it is the bottom and not the top who describes the experience in spiritual terms.[24]

Rethinking the "Omnis" as Divine Drag

Finally, the doctrine of God can be viewed as radical love to the extent that it dissolves the boundaries that prevent us from rethinking God's divine attributes in queer ways. The God of classical theism is described as having all-powerful "omni" characteristics such as omniscience (all-knowing), omnipotence (all-powerfulness), and omnibenevolence (all-goodness). For some queer theologians, this traditional understanding of God is toxic. For example, Robert Williams encouraged LGBT people to "fire" the God of their childhood, which often can be abusive and demonic. Instead, Williams argued that we must try on new models of God, including God as female, as grandmother, as divine lover, and as the one who suffers with us.[25]

As an HIV-positive man, Williams rejected the view of an omnipotent and all-powerful God, which Dorothee Sölle has described as "sadomasochistic" spirituality (and not in a good way).[26] Williams refused to believe that an all-powerful God could allow the horrific suffering of HIV/AIDS to exist. To think otherwise—that is, to worship a God who doesn't need humans and is unmoved by our sorrows and joys—is "psychologically and spiritually unhealthy."[27] J. Michael Clark, an openly gay theologian living with HIV/AIDS, also has wrestled with such questions of theodicy (that is, how evil can exist with an all-powerful and all-loving God). Clark also documents his battle with HIV/AIDS and challenges the classical theistic understanding of God.[28]

---

[24] Thomas V. Peterson, "Gay Men's Spiritual Experience in the Leather Community," in *Gay Religion*, ed. Scott Thumma and Edward R. Gray (Walnut Creek, CA: AltaMira Press), 347.
[25] Williams, *Just as I Am*, 96.
[26] Williams, *Just as I Am*, 96. (citing Dorothee Sölle).
[27] Williams, *Just as I Am*, 100.
[28] J. Michael Clark, *Defying the Darkness: Gay Theology in the Shadows* (Cleveland, OH: Pilgrim Press, 1997), 27–42.

Malcolm Edwards, a self-described gay post-liberal theologian, has suggested that LGBT people should rethink the God of classical theism. According to Edwards, God's omnipotence does not mean a God who can do anything (such as magically eliminate the HIV/AIDS virus), but rather that "there is nothing which is not in God's providential care." And to say that God is unchanging is not to say that God is apathetic, but rather that "God cannot cease to be good and goodness cannot cease to be all-powerful and all-knowing." Indeed, God's love is different from human love in that it "cannot be taken away." Finally, changelessness, according to Edwards, is not an "inability to act," but rather "faithfulness or steadfastness in God's interactions."[29]

Perhaps a more satisfying way of thinking about God's divine attributes, however, is that such attributes are actually a matter of performativity. Thus, like gender, God's divine attributes are simply a matter of divine performance—a parody or divine drag show—as opposed to characteristics that are "natural" or "essential" for God. This view of God's divine attributes would allow God to take on other "omnis" such as being omnisexual, omnigendered, or omniqueer. As B.K. Hipsher, an ordained minister with the Metropolitan Community Churches, has argued, "We are compelled to image God in the ever-changing, shifting, diverse and multiple transgender realities that human beings embody."[30]

In the end, even viewing the divine attributes as a divine drag show may not be queer enough for describing God. As Gerard Loughlin has noted, God is fundamentally queer because, like the term "queer," God is fundamentally "an identity without existence." In other words, God is "radically unknowable." As Thomas Aquinas has argued, we can only know God by what God is *not*. According to Thomas, we can only say that God is "pure actuality"; God simply *is*.[31] And that is precisely what queerness is—queerness is also "an identity without existence."

---

[29] Stuart et al., *Religion Is a Queer Thing*, 73–74.
[30] B.K. Hipsher, "God Is a Many Gendered Thing: An Apophatic Journey to Pastoral Diversity," in Althaus-Reid and Isherwood, *Trans/formations*, 99.
[31] Loughlin, "Introduction," 10.

As David Halperin describes it, queerness "demarcates not a positivity but a positionality vis-à-vis the normative."[32] We cannot define queerness, but we can "point to the effects of its deployment."[33] So, to the extent that God cannot be described in positive terms, but only by its "positionality" or effects, God is truly queer.

Study Questions

1. How do you think about God? What images come to mind when you think about God? What emotions and/or feelings?

2. What does it mean to say that God is radical love itself? Have you experienced God as love and, if so, what was the experience like?

3. In what ways have queer theologians parodied God's omnipotence as a divine "top"? How does it feel to have God described as the top in a sadomasochistic relationship with humans?

4. Do you agree with theologians like J. Michael Clark who believe that the traditional God of Christian theism is "toxic" for LGBT people?

5. Why would an all-loving and all-powerful God allow natural evil such as HIV/AIDS and moral evil such as anti-LGBT violence to occur?

For Further Study

God
- Clark, *Defying the Darkness*, 27–42 ("Querying the Divine").
- Heyward, *Touching Our Strength*.
- Hipsher, "God Is a Many Gendered Thing."
- Jennings, "YHWH as Erastes."
- Loughlin, "Introduction."
- Loughlin, "Omphalos."
- Stuart, *Religion Is a Queer Thing*, 73–74.

---

[32] Loughlin, "Introduction," 9 (citing David M. Halperin, *Saint Foucault: Towards a Gay Hagiography* ([New York:.Oxford University Press, 1995]), 62).
[33] Loughlin, "Introduction," 10.

Trinity: Internal Community of Radical Love

What relevance does the Trinity have for queer people today? For Christians, the doctrine of the Trinity—that is, God is simultaneously one *and* three—is both a mystery and an expression of the essential truth about God's relational nature. Since the early church councils at Nicea and Constantinople, Christian theology has recognized that God's self is made up of three co-equal and co-eternal persons: (1) God the begetter or the "Father"; (2) God the begotten or the "Son"; and (3) God the procession or the "Holy Spirit." However, God is not three separate persons, but rather one being in three persons. The truth of oneness-in-threeness is expressed in the ancient creeds of the church, including the Nicene Creed.

The doctrine of the Trinity is a manifestation of God's radical love because it is an *internal community of radical love*. That is, the Trinity breaks down a number of categories, including the self and the other. Because God is an *internal* community within God's very being, this collapses the usual difference between the self and the other (that is, otherness as being "external" to one's self). Thus, God consists of both the "self" *and* the "other." Indeed, the love among the three persons of the Trinity has been described by the term *perichōrēsis* (or *circumincessio* in Latin), which means an ecstatic dance or interpenetration of the three persons.[34] Indeed, this relationship is so intimate that it might be thought of in terms of a fluid-bonded polyamorous three-way relationship.

Breaking Down Sexual and Nonsexual Relationships

In addition to breaking down the traditional categories of "self" and "other," the doctrine of the Trinity challenges a binary view of sexual and nonsexual relationships. We are taught from a young age that there are only two kinds of relationships: sexual and nonsexual. The former is pair-bonded, is monogamous, and intended for reproduction. The latter consists of many parties, is nonexclusive, and is intended for friendship.

---

[34] For a Christian theology on "dancing with God," see Jay Emerson Johnson, *Dancing with God: Anglican Christianity and the Practice of Hope* (Harrisburg, PA: Morehouse Publishing, 2005).

This is why antigay Christians view the only acceptable sexual relationship to be heterosexual marriage between one man and one woman; such a marriage is the only relationship that fits the above definition of a sexual relationship. All other relational configurations—from same-sex monogamous couples to polyamorous relationships to hook-up buddies to partners at a sex club—fall outside of this definition and thus are forbidden.

For Elizabeth Stuart, the Trinity is worth reclaiming by queer theologians because, at its heart, the Trinity represents God as passionate friendship. This principle of *passionate friendship* should be at the core of queer theology and ethics because it breaks down the artificial divide between sexual relationships and nonsexual relationships. In other words, passionate friendship displaces pair-bonded, monogamous, reproductive sexuality as the norm for Christian relationships. This is actually consistent with the ideals of early Christian communities, which were grounded in passionate friendship within the body of Christ, and *not* biological families.

According to Stuart, we Christians are called to be promiscuous with our friendship. The Trinity reinforces this ideal of passionate friendship because, as we've seen, God's very own being centers around the radical "dance" and relationships between the three persons of the Godhead. The Trinity itself is a community of passionate friendship, and thus it is a model of how we relate to each other. Furthermore, we Christians are not excluded from this divine community of friends. Quite the contrary! Because we are part of the body of Christ (that is, the second person of the Trinity), we ourselves are drawn into the Trinity itself right here on earth.[35]

Gavin D'Costa, a theologian at the University of Bristol, has a similar view of the relational nature of the Trinity. D'Costa argues that, metaphorically speaking, queer relationships are at the ontological heart of the Trinity. D'Costa draws upon Hans von Balthasar's theology in which von Balthasar has conceived of each person in the Trinity as both pure act and pure receptivity. That is, each of the three persons of the Trinity is simultane-

---

[35] Stuart, *Just Good Friends*, 240–44.

ously supramasculine *and* suprafeminine in its own giving and receiving, which spills forth into the universe.[36]

D'Costa's view of the Trinity has some very radical implications. First, both transgender and "switch" (that is, "versatile" or both "top" and "bottom") relationships are at the very heart of the Trinity. That is, each person in the divine three-way is both male and female as well as top and bottom. Thus, queer relationships are divinely sanctioned as long as such relationships also represent an overflowing love to the wider community. Second, the transgender nature of the Trinity means that, as an ontological matter, women should be permitted to be ordained Roman Catholic priests. That is, Roman Catholic theology traditionally asserts that only men can be ordained priests because Jesus Christ was ontologically male. However, under D'Costa's view of the Trinity, the second person of the Trinity—Jesus Christ—is ontologically both male *and* female. Therefore, there would be no theological bar to ordaining women as Roman Catholic priests.[37]

Breaking Down Pair-Bonded Relationships

In addition to passionate friendship, the doctrine of the Trinity can be understood in other, even more radical ways. For example, Marcella Althaus-Reid views the Trinity as a critique of both heterosexuality and monogamy. Althaus-Reid argues that the relationships within the Trinity should be understood as pointing to an emptying, or *kenosis,* of the heterosexual monogamous God. Althaus-Reid calls this an "omnisexual kenosis," that is, the process by which God is revealed as a gender-fluid and polyamorous being, which reflects the three-way relationship that is at the heart of the Trinity. Furthermore, this process of omnisexual kenosis also challenges the heterosexual constructions and readings of LGBT sexualities.

For Althaus-Reid, the Trinity needs to be understood as an orgy, which breaks down the privileging of binary or pairbonded relationships. Initially, the Trinity appears to be an

---

[36] For an alternative view of von Balthasar and the Trinity, see Linn Marie Tonstad, "Sexual Difference and Trinitarian Death: Cross, Kenosis, and Hierarchy in the Theo-Drama," *Modern Theology* 26, no. 4 (October 2010): 603–31.

[37] See Gavin D'Costa, "Queer Trinity," in Loughlin, *Queer Theology,* 272–79; see also Goss, *Queering Christ,* 36–55 ("Catholic Anxieties Over (Fe)Male Priests").

example of "restricted polyfidelity" in which the three persons of the Godhead are themselves in a closed, or faithful, sexual relationship. However, Althaus-Reid argues that each person of the Trinity has her/her own closet of lovers and "forbidden desires" (for example, Jesus' relationships with Mary Magdalene and Lazarus), which in turn results in the death of the "illusion of limited relationships." For Althaus-Reid, the Trinity reminds us that men and women are not limited to "dyadic" or "fixed" sexual identities, but rather "multitudes."[38]

As such, the Trinity can be a model for individuals who are polyamorous because the Trinity deconstructs the binary relationship model of marriage and domestic partnerships.[39] Indeed, the radical love of the Trinity dissolves the boundaries between coupledom and singleness. Also, to the extent that each of the three persons of the Trinity are multigendered—as argued by Gavin D'Costa above—then the Trinity is actually a polygendered or polysexual being itself!

Breaking Down Fragmented Identities

An important principle in contemporary Trinitarian theory is that each of the three persons of the Trinity are present in the external works of God. For example, the biblical witness shows that each of the three persons of the Trinity were present at the moment of creation.[40] In other words, the internal life of the Trinity is expressed in the external works of the Trinity. Thus, gay theologian Daniel Helminiak has argued, the Trinity is reflected in the external life of the LGBT community. Specifically, Helminiak argues that both the Trinity and the LGBT community are characterized by four factors: (1) friendships beyond gender limitation, (2) equality in relationships, (3) personal growth, and (4) preservation of personal uniqueness.[41]

For me, as an openly gay Asian American person of faith, I believe that my life—as well as the lives of other LGBT people

---

[38] Althaus-Reid, *The Queer God*, 57–59.

[39] In fact, the Bible contains at least forty different kinds of family relationships. See Virginia Ramey Mollenkott, *Sensuous Spirituality: Out from Fundamentalism* (New York: Crossroad, 1992), 194–97. For a theological discussion of polyamory, see Robert E. Goss, "Proleptic Sexual Love: God's Promiscuity Reflected in Christian Polyamory," *Theology and Sexuality* 11, no. 1 (Sept. 2004): 52–63.

[40] See Gen. 1–2; John 1:1.

[41] Daniel A. Helminiak, *Sex and the Sacred: Gay Identity and Spiritual Growth* (Binghamton, NY: Harrington Park Press, 2006), 132–36.

of color who are self-identified as spiritual or religious—is a reflection of the inner life of the Trinity. All too often, we are forced to separate our sexual, racial, and spiritual identities into separate compartments. For example, with respect to sexuality, it is difficult to be openly gay in many Asian American communities and/or faith communities, both of which can be highly homophobic. With respect to race, it is difficult to openly embrace one's Asian American heritage in many LGBT communities and/or faith communities, both of which can be highly racist. Finally, with respect to spirituality, it is difficult to be an "out" person of faith in many LGBT communities and/or Asian American communities, both of which can be very secular and have a deep bias against religion and spirituality.[42]

By contrast, the divine interpenetration of the three persons of the Trinitarian Godhead helps us to weave together each of the strands of our often-fragmented identities as LGBTQ people of color who are spiritually identified. In other words, *perichōrēsis* or *circumincessio* is an ideal way of describing the interrelated dance between the three identities of sexuality, race, and spirituality. We are whole only when we can embrace all three of these identities.[43] Furthermore, because these identities are fluid and interpenetrate each other, a Trinitarian conception of queer identity is helpful in responding to any objections queer theorists might have with respect to talking about the "fixed" nature of sexual, racial, and spiritual identities.

---

[42] For some perspectives on the queer Asian American spiritual experience, see Patrick S. Cheng, "Hybridity and the Decolonization of Asian American and Queer Theologies," *Postcolonial Theology Network*, entry posted October 17, 2009, http://www.facebook.com/topic.php?uid=23694574926&topic=11026; Patrick S. Cheng, "Galatians," in Guest et al., *Queer Bible Commentary*, 624–29; Cheng, "Multiplicity and Judges 19"; Cheng, "Reclaiming Our Traditions, Rituals, and Spaces"; Cheng, "Rethinking Sin and Grace for LGBT People Today"; Patrick S. Cheng, Response to "Same-Sex Marriage and Relational Justice," *Journal of Feminist Studies in Religion* 20, no. 2 (2004): 103–7; Patrick S. Cheng, Review of *Queering Christ: Beyond Jesus Acted Up*, by Robert E. Goss, *Union Seminary Quarterly Review* 57, nos. 1–2 (2003): 158–60; Michael Kim, "Out and About: Coming of Age in a Straight White World," in *Asian American X: An Intersection of 21st Century Asian American Voices*, ed. Arar Han and John Hsu (Ann Arbor: University of Michigan Press, 2004), 139–48 (written under a pseudonym); Eric H.F. Law, "A Spirituality of Creative Marginality," in Comstock and Henking, *Que(e)rying Religion*, 343–36; Jeanette Mei Gim Lee, "Queerly a Good Friday," in *Restoried Selves: Autobiographies of Queer Asian/Pacific American Activists*, ed. Kevin K. Kumashiro (Binghamton, NY: Harrington Park Press, 2004), 81–86; Leng Leroy Lim, "'The Bible Tells Me to Hate Myself': The Crisis in Asian American Spiritual Leadership," *Semeia* 90/91 (2002): 315–22; Leng Leroy Lim, "Exploring Embodiment," in *Boundary Wars: Intimacy and Distance in Healing Relationships*, ed. Katherine Hancock Ragsdale (Cleveland, OH: Pilgrim Press, 1996), 58–77; Leng Leroy Lim, "Webs of Betrayal, Webs of Blessings," in *Q&A: Queer in Asian America*, ed. David L. Eng and Alice Y. Hom (Philadelphia: Temple University Press, 1998), 323–34; Leng Lim, Kim-Hao Yap, and Tuck-Leong Lee, "The Mythic-Literalists in the Province of South Asia," in *Other Voices, Other Worlds: The Global Church Speaks Out on Homosexuality*, ed. Terry Brown (New York: Church Publishing, 2006), 58–76.

[43] See Patrick S. Cheng, "A Three-Part Sinfonia: Queer Asian Reflections on the Trinity," in *New Overtures*, ed. Eleazar Fernandez (Louisville, KY: Sopher Press, 2011) (forthcoming).

In sum, the doctrine of the Trinity underscores the fact that God's very own being is an internal community of radical love. By being both three and one, a Trinitarian understanding of God dissolves a number of boundaries: the self and the other, public and private relationships, pair-bonded relationships, and fragmented identities. As Christians, we are the body of Christ, and, as such, we are all brought into the Trinity itself and become part of the divine dance of radical love.

Study Questions

1. How do you make sense of the Trinity? What are the implications of understanding the Trinity as an internal community of radical love?

2. What kinds of different relationships have you been part of? How does Stuart's notion of passionate friendship break down the artificial divide between private and public relationships?

3. How does a queer view of the Trinity challenge the notion that Jesus Christ was ontologically male? That is, how might the Trinity be used to argue that women can be ordained as Roman Catholic priests because Jesus was ontologically both male *and* female?

4. How might the Trinity challenge your thinking about polyamorous and non-dyadic sexual relationships?

5. What is the significance of the Trinity for people who exist at the intersections of multiple sexual, racial, and spiritual identities? For example, how might the doctrine of the Trinity speak to LGBT people of color who are spiritually identified?

For Further Study

Trinity
- Althaus-Reid, *Queer God*, 46–59 ("Queering God in Relationships: Trinitarians and God the Orgy").
- Cheng, "A Three-Part Sinfonia."
- D'Costa, "Queer Trinity."
- Helminiak, *Sex and the Sacred*, 129–42 ("The Trinitarian Vocation of the Gay Community").
- Loughlin, "God's Sex."
- Stuart, *Just Good Friends*, 239–47 ("Friend God").

Creation: God's Outpouring of Radical Love

The final topic in this chapter about God is the doctrine of creation. Creation is at the heart of our understanding of God. For example, the Bible begins with the account that, in the beginning, "God created the heavens and the earth" and that God saw that creation was good.[44] In the Nicene Creed, we profess our belief in the God who is the "maker of heaven and earth, of all that is seen and unseen." Even human beings are described as being created in the "image" and "likeness" of God.[45]

So what is the significance of creation for LGBT people today? I believe that creation can be understood as *God's outpouring of radical love*. As we have seen in the previous section about the doctrine of the Trinity, God's own being is inherently relational. That is, because of God's three-fold existence, God is already a self-contained community and does not *need* anything else that is external to Godself. However, God *chooses* to create the universe—including humanity—as an outpouring of God's radical love.

Indeed, this outpouring of radical love is manifested in the lives of queer people every day. Many LGBT people are actively engaged in acts of creation on a daily basis—whether it is playing music, singing, dancing, acting, painting, writing poetry, or even doing theology. Indeed, it is not an exaggeration to say that the performing arts community, including the church musician community, would have been greatly impoverished without the gifts and contributions of queer people through the centuries.

Dissolving the Dualism of Flesh and Spirit

One way in which the doctrine of creation can be understood as an outpouring of God's radical love is how the doctrine of creation dissolves a dualistic view of flesh and spirit. That is, many people throughout the history of the church have held the dualistic view that matter is evil and spirit is good. This

---

[44] Gen. 1:1, 4.
[45] Gen. 1:26.

arises out of the Platonic view that the abstract world of forms is "higher" than the world of matter, which includes our bodies and sexualities. Indeed, some adherents of this dualistic view of matter and spirit—including the Gnostics and the Manicheans in the early church—have argued that the God of the Hebrew Bible is actually evil because of God's role in creating the universe. Even today, women and LGBT people are still seen as less pure by Christians with dualistic tendencies because of our associations with the body and sexuality—as opposed to the spirit.

Christian theology has ultimately rejected this negative view of the flesh in favor of the notion that the God we worship in fact created the universe and did so *ex nihilo* (that is, out of nothing). As such, all matter—including our bodies and sexualities—is a creation of God's and is fundamentally good. For example, gay theologian Donald Boisvert makes this connection between creation and eros. Specifically, Boisvert describes creation as an "evolutionary cosmic orgy."[46] Boisvert cites the work of Teilhard de Chardin, who posited that the entire natural cosmos—that is, all of God's creation—is the body of Christ.

Boisvert said that he had found Teilhard's idea to be "intensely attractive" and "erotically charged" because "we are all making love together, all the time, down through history and far into the distant future." Boisvert translated this idea into homoerotic terms by seeing every other male body as being part of the same cosmic Christ.[47] This insight can be taken even further in terms of viewing all people as erotically connected—regardless of sexuality or gender identity—within creation.[48]

Dissolving the Dualism of Humanity and Creation

Another way in which the doctrine of creation can be understood as God's outpouring of radical love is that it dissolves the dualism, or hierarchical relationship, of human beings and the rest of creation. This is particularly important in light of

---

[46] Donald L. Boisvert, *Sanctity and Male Desire: A Gay Reading of Saints* (Cleveland, OH: Pilgrim Press, 2004), 179.
[47] See Boisvert, *Sanctity and Male Desire*, 179.
[48] Here I refer to Audre Lorde's definition of the erotic as the "sharing of joy, whether physical, emotional, psychic or intellectual" with another person. See Audre Lorde, "Uses of the Erotic: The Erotic as Power," in Ellison and Douglas, *Sexuality and the Sacred*, 75.

the ecological crisis facing the earth, which arises out of the notion that the created order was made for the sole enjoyment of human beings (as opposed to humans beings serving as stewards of the created order).

For example, Daniel T. Spencer proposes an "erotic ethic of ecojustice" in his book *Gay and Gaia* to express the ideal relationship between humanity and creation. For Spencer, the doctrine of creation is uniquely queer because God was not content to create just one kind of creation, but rather an incredibly diverse and multifaceted universe. This diversity of creation counters the fundamentalist and natural law argument that there should only be one kind of relationship because God created only "Adam and Eve, not Adam and Steve." In fact, by observing creation, we see that there are numerous animal species that engage in same-sex and gender variant acts. For example, Bruce Bagemihl, a biologist, has documented in his book *Biological Exuberance* hundreds of animal species that engage in homosexual, bisexual, and transgender behavior, including primates, marine mammals, hoofed mammals, carnivores, marsupials, rodents, bats, waterfowl, shore birds, perching birds, songbirds, flightless birds, reptiles, fishes, and insects.[49]

Spencer's ethical and theological project is to reintegrate the erotic with the ecological. He names several themes that are not only important to LGBT people, but also to an ecological ethic: (1) the centrality of embodiment, (2) valuing diversity at all levels, (3) overcoming disposability and dispensability, and (4) recognizing the danger of appropriating resources without reciprocity.[50] In the end, this ethic of "Gay and Gaia" encourages LGBT people to reexamine their patterns of consumption as well as their relationships with each other and with animals (for example, even with respect to the use of leather in the BDSM community). Spencer encourages LGBT people to "[c]ontinue the Creation, further the joy, and make the horizon become a beautiful image of Creation's grandeur."[51]

---

[49] Bagemihl, *Biological Exuberance*, 263–670 ("A Wondrous Bestiary: Portraits of Homosexual, Bisexual, and Transgendered Wildlife").
[50] See Spencer, *Gay and Gaia*, 339–40.
[51] Spencer, *Gay and Gaia*, 366.

J. Michael Clark also proposes a gay ecotheology that sets out the ideal relationship between humanity and creation. Clark contends that the LGBT experience of "oppression and exclusion" allows us to be aware of the "patterns of domination" in our lives as well as our "domination of nonhuman nature." This includes a sensitivity not only to the violence that is inflicted upon us, but also the violence that society inflicts upon nature and natural resources.[52] For Clark, the rainbow covenant of the ninth chapter of Genesis is a symbol of LGBT solidarity with all other oppressed peoples, including the god/ess and earth.[53] This is what Clark calls an "ecological ethics of interdependence and interconnectedness."[54]

Finally, even a theology of angels and demons serves to dissolve the dualism between human beings and creation. Angels and demons have particular significance for LGBT people in that many of us are taught from a young age that we will suffer the torments of Satan, demons, and hell if we engage in same-sex or gender-variant behavior. Furthermore, the Sodom narrative in Genesis 19—which is at the root of much theological homophobia and heterosexism—involves the punishment of the cities of Sodom and Gomorrah for the attempted rape of two disguised angels by the cities' male inhabitants.[55]

As such, it is important for LGBT people to reclaim the doctrine of angels and demons and to understand them as more than just agents of divine punishment. To the extent that angels and demons traditionally are understood to be part of the created order, they remind human beings that we are *not* the center around which the universe revolves. For example, Donald Boisvert writes about his erotic connection with Michael the Archangel as the perfect "manly angel" who is the "strong, silent type" (as opposed to "emasculated" angels who nowadays are seen as "harmless guides and messengers"). Boisvert notes how angels are attractive because they occupy

[52] J. Michael Clark, *Beyond Our Ghettos: Gay Theology in Ecological Perspective* (Cleveland, OH: Pilgrim Press, 1993), 12–13.

[53] Clark, *Beyond Our Ghettos*, 41–42.

[54] Clark, *Beyond Our Ghettos*, 55.

[55] See Jude 1:7, which condemns the pursuit by such inhabitants of *heteras sarkos* or, literally, "other flesh."

the liminal space of "in-betweenness" between the divine and human.[56] As such, angels remind human beings that there is more to the universe than just humans and the visible created order.

Robert Williams has written about the role of Satan and demons in the life of LGBT people. For Williams, it is possible to believe in demons without giving up a scientific view of the universe. That is, we must adopt a worldview that sees sickness and disease as "manifestations of the demonic forces that are alive and virulent in our world." For Williams, these forces do not belong to the realm of creation, but rather the "realm of the Fall."[57] That is, evil does not have an independent existence as part of God's creation, but rather is the privation of good. Again, this helps to remind human beings that there is more to the universe than just humans and the visible created order.

Dissolving the Dualism of Marriage and Queer Sex

Finally, the doctrine of creation can be understood as an outpouring of radical love to the extent that it dissolves the dualism between marriage and queer (that is, nonprocreative) sex. Christian theology has traditionally viewed marriage and queer sex as mutually exclusive categories. Because God created "Adam and Eve, not Adam and Steve," antigay Christians have argued that marriage can only occur between one man and one woman. However, queer theologians have challenged this view based upon their view of the doctrine of creation.

For example, the openly gay theologian Eugene F. Rogers argues that creation is an act of pure grace on the part of God. God does *not* need to engage in the act of creation because God is already a self-sustaining community of love in the Trinity (that is, God contains the "otherness" that is required for love within Godself). God is under no compulsion to create the cosmos and human beings. Thus, creation is a pure act of grace and unmerited love.[58]

---

[56] Boisvert, *Sanctity and Male Desire*, 37.

[57] Williams, *Just as I Am*, 165.

[58] Eugene F. Rogers, *Sexuality and the Christian Body: Their Way into the Triune God* (Oxford, UK: Blackwell Publishers, 1999), 199.

If God is under no compulsion to engage in creation, then human beings are also under no compulsion to procreate in order to fulfill the image and likeness of God. Just as creation is an act of pure grace on the part of God, so is procreation. As such, marriage need not be restricted to one man and one woman. Unmerited self-giving love is at the heart of all forms of committed relationships, not procreation.[59]

In sum, not only is creation a function of God's overflowing radical love, but it also dissolves the dualism between matter and spirit, between human beings and the rest of the creation, and between marriage and queer sex. Creation is much more than God's affirmation of procreation. Creation is about the radical love that spills out of the Trinity and overflows into the created order. God brings us into existence as a result of pure grace. As such, God's grace is at the heart of the doctrine of creation, and queer relationships bear witness to such grace.

[59] Similarly, Elizabeth Stuart notes that baptism, like creation, is a "purely gratuitous gift" based upon God's love for us. See Elizabeth Stuart, "Sacramental Flesh," in Loughlin, *Queer Theology*, 67.

Study Questions

1. How can creation be understood as God's outpouring of radical love? Why does God not *need* creation?

2. What are some ways in which you have been blessed with gifts of creativity? How has the LGBT community been blessed with gifts of creativity?

3. How does creation dissolve the dualism of flesh and spirit?

4. What is an erotic ethic of ecojustice? How does the diversity of creation affirm the variety of LGBT sexualities?

5. How might one argue that, theologically speaking, procreation is *not* required for marriage and thus same-sex marriages should be recognized?

6. How have queer theologians thought about angels and demons, and what is the relationship of these creatures to the doctrine of creation?

For Further Study

Creation

Creation
- Clark, *Beyond Our Ghettos.*
- Rogers, *Sexuality and the Christian Body*, 195–218 ("Creation, Procreation, and the Glory of the Triune God").
- Spencer, *Gay and Gaia.*

Angels
- Boisvert, *Sanctity and Male Desire*, 25–38 ("Michael the Archangel").

Demons
- Williams, *Just as I Am*, 161–66 ("Giving the Devil Its Due").

Chapter Four

Jesus Christ:
The Recovery of Radical Love

Having discussed the doctrine of God as the sending forth of radical love, we now proceed to the doctrine of Jesus Christ, the second person of the Trinity. Who is Jesus Christ for LGBT people today? What does it mean to be saved? This chapter proposes that, for queer people, Jesus Christ can be understood as the one who *recovers radical love* for us.

As noted previously, radical love is defined as a love that is so extreme that it dissolves all kinds of boundaries, including those relating to gender and sexuality. Although God is constantly sending forth radical love in the act of creation, sin can be understood as our refusal to accept this radical love. That is, the condition of original sin encourages humans to build up existing boundaries and divisions, and refuse to dissolve them or tear them down. In this framework, Jesus Christ is the one who helps us to recover the radical love that we have rejected.

This chapter will discuss four classical doctrines relating to Jesus Christ. The first doctrine is that of *sin*, which is the distancing of ourselves from God. The second doctrine is that of *Jesus Christ*, which is the embodied means by which God brings us back to radical love. The third doctrine is that of *Mary*, who is the God-bearer and one who says "yes" in giving herself to God. The fourth and final doctrine is that of *atonement*, or how we are reconciled—that is, how we become "at-one"—with God.

Sin: Rejection of Radical Love

Sin is a very difficult topic for many LGBT people. Many of us have grown up being told that we are sinners and that we will go to hell for our nonconforming sexualities and/or gender identities. It is not surprising, therefore, that the doctrine of sin has not received a lot of attention in queer theology to date.[1] Indeed, much of the discussion around sin and LGBT people has been focused on biblical interpretation and the handful of "texts of terror" relating to same-sex acts and nonconforming gender behavior. This approach is what I call the legalistic approach to sin: if you break God's biblical or natural law, then you will be punished for it.

In contrast to the legalistic approach to sin, this section proposes that sin can better be understood as the *rejection of radical love*. That is, if God is radical love (in other words, a love so extreme that it dissolves all kinds of boundaries), then sin is what opposes God, or what opposes radical love. Sin is the resistance to dissolving boundaries and divisions. Specifically, we sin when we reinforce existing divisions with respect to sexuality, gender identity, or other factors. Before exploring this view of original sin, however, it is important to review briefly the traditional doctrine of sin, which some queer theologians have found useful.

Traditional Doctrine of Sin as Disobedience

The traditional doctrine of sin is a legalistic one. That is, sin is defined as disobedience with respect to God's divine commands. Under this view, original sin is attributed to the fall of Adam and Eve, who disobeyed God's command not to eat of the Tree of the Knowledge of Good and Evil.[2] As a result, God punishes Adam and Eve by expelling them from Eden and by introducing death into the world. Augustine of Hippo, in his reading of the Letter to the Romans, argued that this "original sin" of Adam and Eve tainted all of humanity subsequently and was passed on from generation to generation through sexual acts. It is only through the three goods of marriage (fidelity, procreation, and sacrament) that sexual acts can be redeemed. Furthermore, is only through the life, death, and resurrection

---

[1] See, e.g., Dawne Moon, *God, Sex, and Politics: Homosexuality and Everyday Theologies* (Chicago: University of Chicago Press, 2004), 89 (noting how pro-LGBT Christians often fail to "challenge head-on the argument that homosexuality was sinful" and "dodge the question").

[2] Although both Adam and Eve had disobeyed God's command, Adam blames Eve for tempting him, see Gen. 3:12, and the Western theological tradition has subsequently blamed Eve as well as all women for original sin. See Gale Yee, *Poor Banished Children of Eve: Women as Evil in the Hebrew Bible* (Minneapolis, MN: Fortress Press, 2003), 59–79 (citing Sir. 25:24, 1 Tim. 2:11–15).

of Jesus Christ—who is the second Adam—that the punishment for original sin is reversed.

This legalistic view of sin leads to the privileging of pride and disobedience as the root causes of sin. It also leads to a negative view of sexuality, which is understood as the means by which original sin is passed on from generation to generation and thus only can be redeemed through the procreative act. As many feminist theologians have argued, the main issue for many women—and, I would argue, LGBT and other oppressed people—is not that they have too much pride, but rather they do not have *enough* pride. That is, sin takes the form of hiding or running away from the gifts that God has given us. Instead of pride, sin takes the form of shame, or the inability to lift oneself up high enough.[3]

Some queer theologians, however, have embraced the traditional doctrine of original sin, particularly to the extent that it dissolves the simplistic boundaries between morally "good" versus morally "bad" people. According to those theologians, one of the most powerful implications of original sin for LGBT people is that it is a radical equalizer; no one is exempt from the clutches of original sin. Thus, it makes no sense to view LGBT people as particularly egregious sinners deserving of special condemnation because, in the end, *we are all equally fallen*. James Alison, an openly gay Roman Catholic theologian, has noted that the real significance of original sin is that "we are all in the same boat as regards wickedness, and that it is a really terrible thing to do to judge others, because in doing so we become blind to the way we are judging ourselves."[4] Similarly, Robert Williams has noted: "Original sin means that we all, without exception, suffer from a diminished capacity to love. We hurt each other because it is in our very nature to do so; we wound each other because we are all wounded, because we are all literally 'living in sin.'"[5]

Other queer theologians have tried to preserve the traditional doctrine of sin by focusing on systemic or societal sin.

---

[3] See Cheng, "Rethinking Sin and Grace for LGBT People Today," 108.

[4] James Alison, "The Gay Thing: Following the Still Small Voice," in Loughlin, *Queer Theology*, 60.

[5] Williams, *Just as I Am*, 165–66.

Again, this view ends up dissolving the boundaries between "good" versus "bad" people because we are *all* caught up in the clutches of systemic sin. J. Michael Clark notes that, rather than being focused on the sinfulness of particular sexual acts, we should pay more attention to the "systemic or structural foundations of oppression, exploitation, and expendability." This includes not only systematic sins such as racism, sexism, and heterosexism, but also "ecological misdeeds," which Clark defines as "rejecting one's responsibility toward all things within the interconnected web of being." For Clark, original sin is the "very anthropomorphism, human arrogance, or egocentrism that permeates our culture and society."[6]

Sin as Essentialism, or the Rejection of Radical Love

In my article, "Rethinking Sin and Grace for LGBT People," I have proposed an alternative to the traditional legalistic notion of sin. In particular, I have argued that a better way to think about sin—for LGBT people as well as everyone else—is to define sin as our opposition to what God has done for us in Jesus Christ. That is, rather than relying on a legalistic system of rules and laws, we shift our focus back to Jesus Christ.[7] For example, to the extent that God lifts up humanity in the resurrection of Jesus Christ, then sin can be understood to be shame, or the refusal to be lifted up and to take our rightful place as people who are made in the image and likeness of God. This is consistent with feminist notions of sin as hiding or running away from God. For LGBT people, this takes the form of the closet. Only grace in the form of coming out can set us free. (I have argued elsewhere that other forms of sin for LGBT people include exploitation, apathy, conformity, and singularity. By contrast, the corresponding forms of grace for LGBT people may include mutuality, activism, transgression, and hybridity.)[8]

To the extent that we understand God as radical love, or a love so extreme that it dissolves existing boundaries, then we can also understand sin as *that which opposes radical love*. What

6 Clark, *Beyond Our Ghettos*, 69.
7 See Cheng, "Rethinking Sin and Grace for LGBT People Today," 107–8.
8 See generally Cheng, "Rethinking Sin and Grace for LGBT People Today."

would this look like? In the context of radical love, we can understand sin as humanity's rejection of the radical love that God has given to us. In other words, if radical love is understood as a love so extreme that it dissolves existing boundaries, then the rejection of radical love is *essentialism*, or the reinforcing of the boundaries that keep categories separate and distinct from each other.

Take, for example, the issue of sexuality. Queer sexuality can be understood as dissolving traditional categories of homosexuality and heterosexuality. That is, bisexuality creates a third space that destabilizes these two polar identities. Sin in this context (that is, a rejection of radical love) would be the refusal to challenge these two binary categories and to reinscribe the essentialist notions of sexuality as being either homosexuality or heterosexuality! Similarly, queer gender identity can be understood as dissolving traditional categories of female and male. In that context, transgender identity is the third space that destabilizes these categories.

Put differently, sin can be understood by queer theology to be *sexual and gender essentialism*. That is, whenever we understand sexuality and gender identity to be fixed and unchangeable (that is, by limiting sexuality to only homosexual and heterosexual, or by limiting gender identity to only female and male), we commit the sin of essentialism by failing to recognize the constructed nature of these categories. In creating and perpetuating these false dichotomies, we reinforce—rather than erase—sexual and gender categories. By contrast, whenever we challenge the essentialist nature of these categories, we experience the grace of constructivism.

Sin as Separating Race and Sexuality

Another form of sin is the refusal to challenge the boundaries that keep race and sexuality apart (that is, as mutually exclusive categories). In other words, society generally sees the two categories of race and sexuality as mutually exclusive and rarely overlapping. That is, society perpetuates the myth that all people of color are straight (and thus are opposed to LGBT issues), and that all queer people are white (and thus are opposed to issues relating to people of color). This is particularly true when society wants these two groups to be pitted against each other, as has been the case with the marriage equality movement. This, of course, renders queer people of color as nonexistent. A theology of radical love would challenge sin as the race-sexuality boundary and focus on the ways in which these boundaries can be dissolved.[9]

Examples of this sin can be found in the writings of queer African American theologians. Renée L. Hill, for example, has written about the ways in which womanist (that is, African American women) theologians have focused on racism and sexism to the exclusion of lesbians.[10] Similarly, Elias Farajajé-Jones has written about the ways in which the African American community has marginalized bisexual people in its midst.[11] Other theologians and ethicists who have written about the complex relationship between race and sexuality in the black community include Lisa Ann Anderson, Robert Beckford, Kelly Brown Douglas, Joan M. Martin, Darnell L. Moore, Anthony B. Pinn, Edward Rodman, and Emilie M. Townes.[12]

In recent years, more voices of openly queer black theologians of color have emerged to challenge the homophobia and heterosexism of African American churches. These include several voices in the anthology *A Whosoever Church: Welcoming Lesbians and Gay Men into African American Congregations.*[13]

---

[9] For an example of dissolving the boundaries between race and sex, see Laurel C. Schneider, "What Race Is Your Sex?," in *Disrupting White Supremacy from Within: White People on What We Need to Do*, ed. Jennifer Harvey, Karin A. Case, and Robin Hawley Gorsline (Cleveland, OH: Pilgrim Press, 2004), 142–62.

[10] See Renee L. Hill, "Who Are We for Each Other?: Sexism, Sexuality and Womanist Theology," in Cone and Wilmore, *Black Theology II*, 345–51.

[11] See Farajajé-Jones, "Breaking Silence," 139–59. See also Victor Anderson, "African American Church Traditions," in Siker, *Homosexuality and Religion*, 48–50.

[12] See Lisa Ann Anderson, "Desiring to Be Together: A Theological Reflection on Friendship Between Black Lesbians and Gay Men," *Theology and Sexuality*, no. 9 (Sept. 1998): 59–63; Robert Beckford, "Does Jesus Have a Penis?: Black Male Sexual Representation and Christology," *Theology and Sexuality*, no. 5 (Sept. 1996): 10–21; Kelly Brown Douglas, *Sexuality and the Black Church: A Womanist Perspective* (Maryknoll, NY: Orbis Books, 1999); Joan M. Martin, *More Than Chains and Toil: A Christian Work Ethic of Enslaved Women* (Louisville, KY: Westminster John Knox Press, 2000), 146–47; Darnell L. Moore, "Theorizing the 'Black Body' as a Site of Trauma: Implications for Theologies of Embodiment," *Theology and Sexuality* 15, no. 2 (May 2009), 175–88; Anthony B. Pinn, *Embodiment and the New Shape of Black Theological Thought* (New York: New York University Press, 2010); Edward Rodman, "A Lost Opportunity?: An Open Letter to the Leadership of the Episcopal Church," in *To Heal the Sin-Sick Soul: Toward a Spirituality of Anti-Racist Ministry*, ed. Emmett Jarrett (New London, CT: Episcopal Urban Caucus, 1996); Emilie M. Townes, "Marcella Althaus-Reid's *Indecent Theology*: A Response," in Isherwood and Jordan, *Dancing Theology in Fetish Boots*, 61–67; Emilie M. Townes, Response to "Same-Sex Marriage and Relational Justice," *Journal of Feminist Studies in Religion* 20, no. 2 (Fall 2004): 100–103.

[13] See Gary David Comstock, *A Whosoever Church: Welcoming Lesbians and Gay Men into African American Congregations* (Louisville, KY: Westminster John Knox Press, 2001).

These voices also include Horace Griffin, who wrote *Their Own Receive Them Not: African American Lesbians and Gays in Black Churches*, and Roger Sneed, who wrote *Representations of Homosexuality: Black Liberation Theology and Cultural Criticism.*[14] Other voices include Ashon T. Crawley, EL Kornegay, and Irene Monroe.[15] Finally, there have been anthologies of writings of LGBT black people of faith, including *Spirited: Affirming the Soul and Black Gay/Lesbian Identity.*[16]

Queer Asian American theologians have also written about the sin of keeping issues of race and sexuality apart. For example, Leng Lim, Eric Law, and I have written about the homophobia and heterosexism of Asian and Asian American churches as well as the racism of LGBT communities.[17] Our allies, such as Kwok Pui-lan and Tat-siong Benny Liew, have also written about such issues.[18] Secular queer Asians have also written about the intersections of race and sexuality in a variety of contexts, including the absence of Asian men from mainstream gay pornography.[19] Queer Latina/o and Latin American voices about these issues include Marcella Althaus-Reid, Martín Hugo

---

[14] See Horace L. Griffin, *Their Own Receive Them Not: African American Lesbians and Gays in Black Churches* (Cleveland, OH: Pilgrim Press, 2006); Roger A. Sneed, *Representations of Homosexuality: Black Liberation Theology and Cultural Criticism* (New York: Palgrave Macmillan, 2010).

[15] See Ashon T. Crawley, "Circum-Religious Performance: Queer(ed) Black Bodies and the Black Church," *Theology and Sexuality* 14, no. 2 (Jan. 2008): 201–22; EL Kornegay, "Queering Black Homophobia: Black Theology as a Sexual Discourse of Transformation," *Theology and Sexuality* 11, no. 1 (Sept. 2004): 29–51; Irene Monroe, "Between a Rock and a Hard Place: Struggling with the Black Church's Heterosexism and the White Queer Community's Racism," in *Out of the Shadows, Into the Light: Christianity and Homosexuality*, ed. Miguel A. De La Torre (St. Louis, MO: Chalice Press, 2009), 39–58.

[16] G. Winston James and Lisa C. Moore, eds., *Spirited: Affirming the Soul and Black Gay/Lesbian Identity* (Washington, D.C.: Redbone Press, 2006).

[17] See Lim, "Bible Tells Me to Hate Myself"; Lim, "Exploring Embodiment"; Lim, "Webs of Betrayal"; Lim, Yap, and Lee, "Mythic Literatists"; Law, "Spirituality of Creative Marginality"; Cheng, "Galatians"; Cheng, "Hybridity and the Decolonization of Asian American and Queer Theologies"; Cheng, "Multiplicity and Judges 19"; Cheng, "Reclaiming Our Traditions, Rituals, and Spaces"; Cheng, Response to "Same-Sex Marriage and Relational Justice"; Cheng, "Rethinking Sin and Grace for LGBT People Today"; Cheng, Review of *Queering Christ*. For a discussion of Asian American evangelical college students, see Rudy V. Busto, "The Gospel according to the Model Minority? Hazarding an Interpretation of Asian American Evangelical College Students," in *New Spiritual Homes: Religion and Asian Americans*, ed. David K. Yoo (Honolulu: University of Hawai'i Press, 1999), 69–87.

[18] See Kwok Pui-lan, "Asian and Asian American Churches," in Siker, *Homosexuality and Religion*, 59–62; Kwok Pui-lan, "Body and Pleasure in Postcoloniality," in Isherwood and Jordan, *Dancing Theology in Fetish Boots*, 31–43; Kwok Pui-lan, *Postcolonial Imagination and Feminist Theology* (Louisville, KY: Westminster John Knox Press, 2005), 100–121; Tat-siong Benny Liew, "(Co)Responding: A Letter to the Editor," in Stone, *Queer Commentary and the Hebrew Bible*, 182–92; Tat-siong Benny Liew, "Queering Closets and Perverting Desires: Cross-Examining John's Engendering and Transgendering Word Across Different Worlds," in *They Were All Together in One Place?: Toward Minority Biblical Criticism*, ed. Randall C. Bailey, Tat-siong Benny Liew, and Fernando F. Segovia (Atlanta, GA: Society of Biblical Literature, 2009), 251–88.

[19] See, e.g., Richard Fung, "Looking for My Penis: The Eroticized Asian in Gay Video Porn," in Eng and Hom, *Q&A*, 115–34. For a discussion of the spiritual aspects of gay pornography, see Ron Long, "A Place for Porn in a Gay Spiritual Economy," *Theology and Sexuality*, no. 11 (March 2002): 21–31. For a discussion of male prostitution in a variety of contexts, including Asia, see Rita Nakashima Brock and Susan Brooks Thistlethwaite, *Casting Stones: Prostitution and Liberation in Asia and the United States* (Minneapolis, MN: Fortress Press, 1996), 331–36.

Córdova Quero, Juan M.C. Oliver, and Margarita Suárez,[20] and allies such as Miguel De La Torre and Ivan Petrella.[21]

In sum, sin can be understood as our refusal to accept God's radical love for us. This can take a number of forms, but especially the form of refusing to dissolve or even challenge existing boundaries that limit our views of sexuality, gender identity, and/or race. Sin can also take the form of refusing to see the interrelatedness of social oppressions; for example, continuing to maintain the lines of division between racism and heterosexism.

Study Questions

1. What is the legalistic approach to sin? What are some problems with the traditional view of sin as disobedience?

2. How can sin be understood as the rejection of radical love? What does it mean to understand sin as essentialism?

3. How have certain queer theologians reclaimed the traditional doctrine of original sin? What does it mean to describe original sin as a "radical equalizer"?

4. What are some examples of sexual and gender essentialism?

5. What is sinful about refusing to recognize the intersections between race and sexuality, particularly within queer communities of color?

6. Describe some of the emerging voices of queer Black, Asian, Asian American, Latina/o, and Latin American theologians.

---

[20] See Althaus-Reid, *Indecent Theology*; Althaus-Reid, *Queer God*; Martín Hugo Córdova Quero, "The Prostitutes Also Go into the Kingdom of God: A Queer Reading of Mary of Magdala," in *Liberation Theology and Sexuality*, ed. Marcella Althaus-Reid (Aldershot, UK: Ashgate, 2006), 81–110; Hugo Córdova Quero, "Risky Affairs: Marcella Althaus-Reid Indecently Queering Juan Luis Segundo's Hermeneutical Circle Propositions," in Isherwood and Jordan, *Dancing Theology in Fetish Boots*, 207–18; Juan M.C. Oliver, "Why Gay Marriage?," *Journal of Men's Studies* 4, no. 3 (1996): 209–24; Margarita Suárez, "Reflections on Being Latina and Lesbian," in Comstock and Henking, *Que(e)rying Religion*, 347–50.

[21] See Miguel A. De La Torre, "Confessions of a Latin Macho: From Gay Basher to Gay Ally," in De La Torre, *Out of the Shadows*, 59–75; Ivan Petrella, "Queer Eye for the Straight Guy: The Making Over of Liberation Theology, A Queer Discursive Approach," in Althaus-Reid, *Liberation Theology and Sexuality*, 33–49.

For Further Study

Sin
- Alison, "The Gay Thing."
- Cheng, "Rethinking Sin and Grace for LGBT People Today."
- Clark, *Beyond Our Ghettos*, 68–70 ("Sin and Judgment").
- Williams, *Just as I Am*, 165–68.

Race, Sexuality, and African Americans
- Anderson, "African American Church Traditions."
- Comstock, *A Whosoever Church*.
- Douglas, *Sexuality and the Black Church*.
- Farajajé-Jones, "Breaking Silence."
- Griffin, *Their Own Receive Them Not*.
- Hill, "Who Are We for Each Other?"
- Sneed, *Representations of Homosexuality*.

Race, Sexuality, and Asian Americans
- Cheng, "Galatians."
- Cheng, "Hybridity and the Decolonization of Asian American and Queer Theologies."
- Cheng, "Multiplicity and Judges 19"
- Cheng, "Reclaiming Our Traditions, Rituals, and Spaces."
- Kwok, "Asian and Asian American Churches."
- Kwok, "Body and Pleasure in Postcoloniality."
- Kwok, Postcolonial Imagination, 100–121 ("Finding Ruth a Home: Gender, Sexuality, and the Politics of Otherness").
- Liew, "Queering Closets and Perverting Desires."
- Lim, "The Bible Tells Me to Hate Myself."
- Lim, "Exploring Embodiment."
- Lim, "Webs of Betrayal, Webs of Blessings."
- Lim, Yap, and Lee, "Mythic Literalists."

Race, Sexuality, Latinas/os, and Latin Americans
- Althaus-Reid, *Indecent Theology*
- Córdova Quero, "The Prostitutes Also Go into the Kingdom of God."
- De La Torre, "Confessions of a Latin Macho."
- Oliver, "Why Gay Marriage?"
- Petrella, "Queer Eye for the Straight Guy."
- Suárez, "Reflections on Being Latina and Lesbian."

Jesus Christ: Embodiment of Radical Love

Who is Jesus Christ for LGBT people today? In some ways, this question is at the very heart of Christian theology. Many queer people see Jesus Christ as a great teacher or prophet who lived two thousand years ago, but they generally have difficulty in thinking about Jesus Christ as one being, or substance, with God. They also have difficulty with christological doctrines such as the virgin birth, the miracles, the resurrection, and the ascension.

This section suggests that Jesus Christ—as well as the challenging christological doctrines above—can be understood by LGBT people as the *embodiment of radical love*, or radical love made flesh. As noted in the first chapter of the Gospel according to John, the "Word became flesh and lived among us."[22] Indeed, God loved us so much that God became human in the person of Jesus Christ. If radical love is understood as a love so extreme that it dissolves boundaries, then Jesus Christ is the living embodiment of the dissolution of boundaries. As such, Jesus Christ is the boundary-crosser extraordinaire, whether this relates to divine, social, sexual, or gender boundaries.

Crossing Divine Boundaries

The story of Jesus Christ as told in the four gospels—that is, the narrative of Jesus Christ's incarnation, ministry, crucifixion, resurrection, and ascension—can be difficult to fathom from a post-Enlightenment perspective. What rational and educated person could ever believe in the virgin birth, the miracles, or the resurrection? However, I believe that these events make perfect sense if they are understood as showing how the boundaries between the divine and the human are forever dissolved in the person of Jesus Christ. Thus, the incarnation and miracles can be understood as the crossing of the divine into the human realm. Conversely, the resurrection and ascension can be understood as the crossing of the human back into the divine realm.

Indeed, the story of Jesus Christ fundamentally changes the relationship between God and humanity. That is why, for Christians, Jesus Christ is considered to be the axis around which all of salvation history turns. No longer are "God" and "humanity" mutually exclusive categories, but they come together in the person of Jesus Christ, the God-human, who is fully divine and fully human. For me, this is the true significance of the christological arguments in the early church.

Crossing Social Boundaries

Jesus Christ's earthly ministry also reinforces the notion of Jesus as the embodiment of radical love and boundary-crossing. Throughout his ministry, Jesus constantly dissolved the religious and social boundaries of his time. He ate with tax collectors, prostitutes, and sinners. He touched "unclean" people such a lepers and bleeding women. He spoke with

---

[22] John 1:14.

social outcasts such as Samaritans. In other words, Jesus Christ dissolved the "holy" boundaries of clean and unclean, holy and profane, and saint and sinner. He challenged the religious and political authorities of his day—to such an extent that he was ultimately put to death.

Robert Shore-Goss writes about this boundary-transgressing Jesus Christ in his first book, *Jesus Acted Up*. Shore-Goss, whose long-term partner Frank died of HIV/AIDS, compares Jesus' actions to those of the radical group ACT-UP (that is, AIDS Coalition To Unleash Power), which took to the streets starting in the late 1980s in order to protest the lack of governmental action with respect to HIV/AIDS as well as the silence of religious institutions like the Roman Catholic Church. Shore-Goss urges LGBT communities to "practice queer visibility actions," which he characterizes as "transgressive and nonviolent acts of civil disobedience" with respect to the churches that "crucify queer Christs in their midst."[23] Similarly, Thomas Bohache, another gay theologian and MCC minister, constructs a queer christology of empowerment that views all of us queer Christians as "anointed Christs" who must stir up and spoil the status quo, which again is about transgressing social boundaries.[24]

Crossing Sexual Boundaries

Thirdly, Jesus Christ is the embodiment of radical love because—in addition to crossing divine and social boundaries—Jesus also crosses sexual boundaries. That is, Jesus' life and ministry can be viewed as dissolving the rigid line between "heterosexual" and "homosexual." Bisexuality is significant because it demonstrates what queer theory, as well as the Kinsey report, has argued—that sexuality is not a binary construct, but rather it is a fluid and evolving phenomenon.

What the concept of bisexuality teaches us is that classifying people by the binary categories of "heterosexual" and "homosexual" is ultimately a social construct (in fact, only dating back to the late nineteenth century) and is no more

---

[23] Goss, *Jesus Acted Up*, 151.
[24] Thomas Bohache, *Christology from the Margins* (London: SCM Press, 2008), 242.

"natural" than classifying people by, say, whether they prefer to leave the toothpaste cap off (as opposed to leaving it on) after brushing their teeth, or whether they prefer to have toilet paper go over (as opposed to under) the roll. This is not to deny the fact that certain people are, as a matter of biology, attracted to one sex over another. However, it is to say that binary categories of classification such as "heterosexual" and "homosexual" are not as "natural" as we might think.

In terms of Jesus Christ's bisexuality, Nancy Wilson raises the interesting possibility that Jesus Christ was sexually attracted to both women and men. She discusses Jesus' household in Bethany—that is, Martha, Mary, and Lazarus—and speculates that Jesus could have been attracted to both sexes. According to Wilson, "the most obvious way to see Jesus as a sexual being is to see him as bisexual in orientation, if not also in his actions."[25] Like Wilson, Robert Williams also raises the possibility that Jesus Christ was sexually attracted to men. Williams cites the controversial discovery of the Secret Gospel of Mark by the scholar Morton Smith[26] and discusses the hypothesis that the mysterious nude young man in Mark 14:51–52 was in fact Jesus' lover.[27]

Marcella Althaus-Reid's Bi/Christ is also a powerful example of the sexual-boundary-crossing Jesus Christ. For Althaus-Reid, bisexuality is not a matter of physical sexual acts, but rather a way of thinking. It doesn't matter to Althaus-Reid whether Jesus Christ was a "transvestite, a butch lesbian, a gay or a heterosexual person." What does matter, however, is the way in which bisexuality rejects "hierarchical, binary constructive organised thought."[28] In other words, bisexuality is contrasted to heterosexuality, which reinforces binaries as opposed to challenging them. For Althaus-Reid, the Bi/Christ challenges either/or thinking and categories.

Laurel Dykstra also writes about the bisexual Christ. For Dykstra, who is a bisexual Christian activist, Jesus is "uniquely

[25] Wilson, *Our Tribe*, 147.
[26] See Morton Smith, *The Secret Gospel: The Discovery and Interpretation of the Secret Gospel According to Mark* (New York: Harper and Row, 1973).
[27] Williams, *Just as I Am*, 118–20.
[28] Althaus-Reid, *Indecent Theology*, 114.

bisexual" in that he embraced the "glorious ambiguity and refus[ed] to be held by purity codes, gay or straight."[29] Instead of being "weak, fickle, traitors, and sellouts" (as portrayed by many lesbians and gay men), bisexual people play an important role in challenging the hierarchical mode of thinking that Althaus-Reid critiques. For Dykstra, bi people challenge— simply by their very existence—a binary view of the world, which includes the "gay-straight" dichotomy held by many lesbians and gay men.[30]

Crossing Gender Boundaries

Finally, Jesus Christ is the embodiment of radical love because Jesus crosses gender boundaries. As Paul writes in his letter to the Galatians, "there is no longer male and female" in Christ Jesus.[31] To that end, a number of theologians have written about the transgender Jesus Christ, or the Jesus Christ who dissolves the boundaries between "female" and "male." As in the case with bisexuality, transgender discourse challenges binary and hierarchical thinking about gender.

For example, Eleanor McLaughlin writes about Jesus as a transvestite, or one who refuses to be "caught" by essentialist categories.[32] According to McLaughlin, the transvestite makes clear the constructed nature of gender categories. Like the cross-dressing Joan of Arc, the transvestite challenges societal norms by making ambiguous what society tries to define rigidly. Cross-dressing is "socially taboo behavior," and it is precisely this kind of behavior in which Jesus engages by ministering to those who were unclean and social outcasts.[33]

Indeed, McLaughlin draws upon the phrase coined by Marjorie Garber—the "Third Thing"—as a symbol of how Jesus destroys the dualities of human and divine, which was at the center of the christological debates of the early church. For McLaughlin, the critical issue today is not so much

[29] Dykstra, "Jesus, Bread, Wine and Roses," 86, 87.
[30] Dykstra, "Jesus, Bread, Wine and Roses," 87. Other recent works on Jesus Christ and same-sex love include Theodore W. Jennings, *The Man Jesus Loved: Homoerotic Narratives from the New Testament* (Cleveland, OH: Pilgrim Press, 2003); and Dale B. Martin, *Sex and the Single Savior: Gender and Sexuality in Biblical Interpretation* (Louisville, KY: Westminster John Knox Press, 2006).
[31] Gal. 3:28.
[32] McLaughlin, "Feminist Christologies," 141.
[33] McLaughlin, "Feminist Christologies," 139–41.

understanding the divine and human natures of Jesus as a metaphysical matter, but rather challenging the binaries of gender that continue to oppress women in the church. Indeed, as McLaughlin notes, Jesus creates a space in which "no one is out of place" because the very notion of gender has been transformed: "Yes human, yes god, yes woman, yes man, yes black, yes white, yes yellow, yes friend, yes stranger . . . yes, yes, yes."[34]

Similarly, Justin Tanis proposes a christology for transgender people. For Tanis, Jesus' life experience parallels that of many trans people. Specifically, Jesus is harassed in the streets as well as alienated by his biological family. Jesus has nowhere to lay his head, just as many trans people are unable to find meaningful employment. And, like Jesus, many trans people are killed for transgressing societal norms by being who they are.

Tanis also has an interesting take on the parallels between Jesus' resurrection and those trans people who complete gender reassignment surgery. Many people who have transitioned feel a "sense of resurrection" in that "one part of them dies and another is reborn in their new gender."[35] According to Tanis, this kind of transitioning allows trans people to participate in the resurrection. Furthermore, like Jesus, posttransition individuals are both "the same and different." That is, they did not "die and return as a wholly different being." Rather, they are transfigured and resurrected in a way that defies easy categorization.[36]

Theologians have also started to write about the intersex Jesus Christ, or the Jesus Christ who has physical attributes (either genitalia or chromosomes) of both sexes. For example, Virginia Mollenkott cites the work of Edward L. Kessel, an emeritus professor of biology at the University of San Francisco, for the proposition that Jesus was intersexed. Specifically, Mollenkott argues that if Jesus' birth was truly a result of a virgin pregnancy, then Jesus' birth would be what biologists call parthenogenetic. This means that Jesus would have two X chromosomes

---

[34] McLaughlin, "Feminist Christologies," 142–44.
[35] Tanis, *Trans-Gendered*, 142.
[36] Tanis, *Trans-Gendered*, 142–43.

(because there would not have been a Y chromosome contributed by a man), which means that Jesus would be chromosomally female yet phenotypically male.

Indeed, Kessel concluded that Jesus was not only a man but "also a woman" and, as such, the "Perfect Human Being."[37] In fact, Mollenkott argues that this view of the intersex Christ is reinforced by the Eastern Orthodox Church's characterization of Jesus' wound in his side as "female genitals" that give birth to his bride, the church, "just as Eve was drawn from the side of Adam."[38] For Mollenkott, the intersex Christ is the most perfect image of God possible. This is because the original "perfect" human being was created in God's image, specifically as both male *and* female.[39] Indeed, Mollenkott argues that the church must let go of an "inaccurate and unjust binary gender construct that does not allow room for a Christ Himself who is also Christ Herself!"[40] Similarly, Susannah Cornwall has written about the connections between theology, intersex people, and the body of Christ in her provocative essay "The *Kenosis* of Unambiguous Sex in the Body of Christ: Intersex, Theology and Existing 'for the Other.'"[41]

Kittredge Cherry, a lesbian writer and Metropolitan Community Church minister, has portrayed Jesus Christ as a bisexual-transgender person who has sexual relationships with the apostle John, Mary Magdalene, as well as a "pan-gendered, omni-erotic" Holy Spirit.[42] In her novel, *Jesus in Love*, Jesus speaks in the first person about his multiple sexual identities: "My nature can't be captured in the confines of human language, either. I switch between being gay, straight, lesbian, bisexual, trisexual. . . . If you want to get technical about my love life, it's masturbation as much as incest, since we're really all one Being. But none of the labels really fit."[43] For Cherry, this bisexual-transgender Christ is "too queer for most churches, but too Christian for most queers."[44]

---

[37] Mollenkott, *Omnigender*, 105–6.
[38] Mollenkott, *Omnigender*, 106.
[39] See Gen. 1:27.
[40] Mollenkott, *Omnigender*, 107.
[41] Susannah Cornwall, "The *Kenosis* of Unambiguous Sex in the Body of Christ: Intersex, Theology and Existing 'for the Other,'" *Theology and Sexuality* 14, no. 2 (2008): 181–99.
[42] Kittredge Cherry, *Jesus in Love* (Berkeley, CA: AndroGyne Press, 2006), 139.
[43] Cherry, *Jesus in Love*, 140.
[44] Cherry, *Jesus in Love*, 11.

In summary, not only did Jesus Christ dissolve divine and social boundaries, but Jesus also crossed sexual and gender boundaries. Indeed, recent queer christological reflection has pointed out how truly radical the church's doctrine about Jesus Christ can be in terms of crossing these boundaries. Elizabeth Stuart notes that, from conception, "Jesus is caught up in the divine queering of sex." For example, Jesus is a "male born of no male matter."[45] As such, Jesus crosses traditional gender boundaries about what it means to be chromosomally male. Graham Ward notes that Jesus' body undergoes a "series of displacements" or physical transitions—from circumcision to transfiguration to crucifixion—that culminate in the resurrection, when the church is birthed out of the "womb" of Jesus' side,[46] which also is a crossing of gender boundaries. Finally, Jesus' body, by incorporating the members of the church after the ascension, ultimately becomes a "multi-gendered body" and, as such, "the body of Christ is queer." For Stuart, it makes no sense to ask if a male savior can save women, or what Jesus Christ's sexual orientation was, because those questions show a failure to truly "understand the nature of the body of Christ";[47] that is, the embodiment of a radical love that dissolves sexual and gender boundaries.[48]

[45] Stuart, "The Priest at the Altar: The Eucharistic Erasure of Sex," 131.
[46] Graham Ward, "The Displaced Body of Jesus Christ," in *Radical Orthodoxy: A New Theology*, ed. John Milbank, Catherine Pickstock, and Graham Ward (London: Routledge, 1999), 163, 174.
[47] Stuart, "Sacramental Flesh," 66.
[48] See also Tricia Sheffield, "Performing Jesus: A Queer Counternarrative of Embodied Transgression," *Theology and Sexuality* 14, no. 3 (May 2008): 233–58.

Study Questions

1. How is Jesus Christ the embodiment of radical love? How have you experienced the embodiment of radical love in your own life?

2. What does it mean to view Jesus Christ as a "boundary-crosser extraordinaire"? What are the divine boundaries that he crossed?

3. How did Jesus Christ cross social boundaries? What kinds of social boundaries have you crossed in your own life? Who are the outcasts and unclean people in our society today?

4. How did Jesus Christ cross sexual boundaries? How do you respond to the bisexual or Bi/Christ?

5. How did Jesus Christ cross gender boundaries? What have queer theologians written about the transgender or intersex Christ?

6. Which of the various queer Christologies discussed in this section appealed to you the most? Why?

For Further Study

Jesus Christ
Queer Christologies
- Bohache, *Christology from the Margins*.
- Goss, *Jesus Acted Up*.
- Goss, *Queering Christ*.
- Kwok, "Touching the Taboo."
- Loughlin, "God's Sex."
- Sheffield, "Performing Jesus."
- Stuart, "Priest at the Altar."
- Stuart, "Sacramental Flesh."
- Ward, "The Displaced Body of Jesus Christ."
- Williams, *Just as I Am*, 111–23 ("Jesus the Christ: Our Elder Brother").

Bisexual Christ
- Althaus-Reid, *Indecent Theology*, 112–20 ("Obscenity no. 1: Bi/Christ").
- Dykstra, "Jesus, Bread, Wine and Roses."
- Wilson, *Our Tribe*, 140–48 ("The Bethany Community: Jesus Loved Mary, Martha, and Lazarus").

Transgender/Intersex Christ
- Cornwall, "The *Kenosis* of Unambiguous Sex in the Body of Christ."
- McLaughlin, "Feminist Christologies."
- Mollenkott, *Omnigender*, 105–7 ("The Christian Doctrine of Jesus' Virgin Birth").
- Tanis, *Trans-Gendered*, 138–43 ("Trans Christology").

Mary: Bearer of Radical Love

Who is the Virgin Mary for LGBT people today? As the mother of Jesus Christ and the *theotokos*, or God-bearer, Mary has long played an important role in the spiritual life of the Christian church. Particularly for Roman Catholics, Mary is much more than a Christmas crèche decoration or a character in the annual Christmas pageant. However, for many queer people, Mary is a symbol of the oppressive celibacy and erotophobia that has been used to persecute LGBT people through the ages. So how can we understand Mary in queer terms?

To the extent that Jesus Christ is the incarnation of radical love, then Mary can be understood as the *bearer of radical love*. Mary's radical love is expressed in her "yes" to God in the incarnation, an event that changed the course of salvation history. However, Mary is also the bearer of radical love because her very existence dissolves traditional boundaries about family life as well as gender. For example, Mary challenges family boundaries to the extent that she is not only both a virgin *and* a mother, but that she also is both the mother *and* the heavenly spouse of her son, Jesus Christ.[49] Furthermore, Mary challenges the boundaries between male and female to the extent that she was depicted as the "Virgin Priest" and a "bishop and sacrificing priest" in the nineteenth century, despite the fact that only men could receive holy orders.[50]

Indeed, the Virgin Mary can be understood as the antithesis of "family values" insofar as she erases the boundaries between the traditional family categories of parent, spouse, and child. This is significant because we can understand Mary as deconstructing gender and family roles, as opposed to merely reinforcing them as the Roman Catholic church and fundamentalist Christians would have us believe. As such, this idea of Mary as the *bearer of radical love* may explain why there has been so much queer theological reflection on Mary.

---

[49] For example, in the Middle Ages, Mary's identity became "increasingly merged with that of the church as Bride of Christ." This led to "lavish and widespread" nuptial imagery of Mary as the "Spouse of the Bridegroom." See Tina Beattie, "Queen of Heaven," in Loughlin, *Queer Theology*, 300,

[50] Stuart, "Priest at the Altar," 133.

Dissolving Sexual Oppression

Before exploring the ways in which Mary dissolves traditional family and gender boundaries, it is important to acknowledge that Mary has been an oppressive doctrine for women, especially in the context of traditional Latin American liberation theologies. According to Marcella Althaus-Reid, women who worship Mary in the context of traditional liberation theologies undergo a "spiritual clitoridectomy" that "mutilat[es] their lust." For Althaus-Reid, the "Virgin and the vulva have become disjoined and separated."[51]

This is problematic, according to Althaus-Reid, because it ignores the reality of poor women in Latin America, for whom virginity is almost never compatible with a life of poverty. Such a life often results in violence, promiscuity, rape, prostitution, and sexual bondage. It is time, according to Althaus-Reid, to make "indecent" the liberation theology that makes Mary a "proto-alien" in her identity as a "stone-walled hymen virgin conceiving by copulating with a kind of divine cloud and giving birth in some unimaginable way." (To the extent that one subscribes to the doctrine of the Immaculate Conception, Mary's mother was similarly odd in that Mary was also "conceived from a cloud.") For Althaus-Reid, Mary is easily the "strangest thing in Christianity."[52]

However, the true act of "queering" or "indecenting" is not simply pointing out such oddities, but rather it requires us to recover the "denied reality" of "authentic, everyday life experiences" of poor women in Latin America, which is precisely what is suppressed and hidden by the traditional liberationist narrative of Mary.[53] True "indecenting" requires us to "recall the clitoris" and envision Mary as one who "conceived by pleasure in her clitoris; by self-given pleasure, perhaps."[54]

---

[51] Althaus-Reid, *Indecent Theology*, 49.
[52] Althaus-Reid, *Indecent Theology*, 71.
[53] Althaus-Reid, *Indecent Theology*, 71.
[54] Althaus-Reid, *Indecent Theology*, 73.

Dissolving Family Boundaries

Notwithstanding the ways that the traditional doctrine about Mary has been oppressive to many women, Mary's very existence is a challenge to the boundaries of "traditional" family relationships. As a pregnant woman who was not yet married, Mary deeply challenged the social norms of her time. As John McNeill has suggested, Mary's status as an unwed mother makes her a sexual outcast. As such, Mary is the ideal person to intercede for those of us who are her "special children"— "all of us queers, fags, dykes, fems, fairies, fruits, transvestites, transsexuals, and all sexual exiles."[55]

Furthermore, Mary radically blurs the boundaries between mother, daughter, and spouse. Because Mary traditionally has been understood to be the *theotokos*, or God-bearer, she is not only a daughter of God, but she is also the mother of God. Furthermore, to the extent that Mary is equated with the church as the Bride of Christ, then Mary is also the spouse to her son, Jesus Christ. These incestuous relationships are reinforced by the theological understanding of Mary as the "New Eve" to Jesus Christ's "New Adam."

Similarly, Graham Ward notes that Jesus Christ's relationship to Mary has been historically described in boundary-transgressing ways. For example, Ward notes that Augustine of Hippo describes Jesus Christ as the "Infant Spouse" who is born from his own "bridal chamber," which happens to be the womb of the Virgin Mary. As a result, according to Ward, this makes the infant boy not just the son, but also the "husband and bridegroom, spouse and prefigured lover of the mother who gives him birth."[56]

Dissolving Rational Boundaries

Tina Beattie, a British Roman Catholic theologian at Roehampton University, summarizes the queerness of Mary nicely in her essay "Queen of Heaven," and she also demonstrates how Mary ultimately dissolves the boundaries between

---

[55] John J. McNeill, *Taking a Chance on God: Liberating Theology for Gays, Lesbians, and Their Lovers, Families, and Friends* (Boston: Beacon Press, 1996), 143.
[56] Ward, "Displaced Body," 164.

the rational and irrational. Beattie notes that Mary is fundamentally queer because she is both the mother of Christ as well
as—in her capacity as the New Eve—the Bride of Christ. As
such, the relationship between Jesus and Mary disrupts traditional notions of family. Jesus is simultaneously son, brother,
bridegroom, and Lord to Mary. According to Beattie, these
paradoxes allow the believer to transcend the discourse of
rationality and enter into the "poetics of devotion and prayer,
through the expression of forbidden desire."[57]

Indeed, by following Mary as a marker of the irrational, we
are led into a space of "radical otherness," which is a "foretaste
of our redemption" and is expressed in the language of "desire
constituted as prayer, poetry, art, music, and carnival."[58] Mary
becomes for us the "matrix" within which we find the "collective expression in whispered, forbidden longings for God."[59]

Beattie notes that the original theological significance
of the virgin birth was to demonstrate the divine nature of
Jesus Christ, as opposed to a sign of Mary's sexual purity.
Furthermore, according to the theology of the early church,
Mary's virginal body—which had escaped the "cycle of sex,
procreation, and death"—was a symbol of the "finite human"
who had been transformed into a "divinized and immortal
being" through *theosis*, or the process of becoming divine.[60] For
Beattie, this conception of a divinized Mary actually challenges
all notions of sexuality, heterosexual or otherwise, as opposed
to reinforcing them through the idea of (hetero)sexual purity.

Dissolving Gender Boundaries

Mary's very existence also challenges the boundaries
between female and male. As a virgin mother, Mary deconstructs the heterosexist theologies of male-female complemen-
tariness that views the husband-wife marital bond as "natural"
or heavenly ordained. As Sojourner Truth once said, the significance of the virgin birth was that man had nothing to do with it.
Indeed, contemporary lesbian icons of Mary have emphasized

[57] Beattie, "Queen of Heaven," 294.
[58] Beattie, "Queen of Heaven," 295.
[59] Beattie, "Queen of Heaven," 302.
[60] Beattie, "Queen of Heaven," 296.

the absence of the male. For example, photographer Elisabeth Ohlson created a wonderful tableau of Mary and Elizabeth as lovers and of the angel Gabriel bringing a test-tube of semen to them.[61]

The virgin birth also challenges the traditional biological boundaries between female and male to the extent that Jesus Christ is viewed as an intersex person. As noted above, Virginia Mollenkott has argued that any child that is truly conceived through a virgin birth, or parthenogenesis, must have XX (that is, female) chromosomes since there is no contribution of a Y chromosome from a man. So to the extent that Jesus Christ is a product of parthenogenesis and is traditionally depicted with male genitals,[62] Jesus Christ is actually an intersex person! This observation is important because intersex theology is an emerging area of queer theology,[63] just as the LGBT community is becoming more aware of the intersex political movement and organizations like the Intersex Society of North America.[64]

Another way in which Mary dissolves gender boundaries is through her challenging of patriarchy by providing a path into the divine female. For example, John McNeill has noted that Mary can be a powerful antidote to the purely paternal image of God that is emphasized in traditional Christian discourse.[65] Similarly, Robert Williams argued that Mary is a way for Christians to connect with the divine goddess. For Williams, it is important to see Mary as a symbol of fertility and motherhood, as opposed to virginity. He argues that the emphasis on Mary's virginity has often resulted in Mary—as well as women generally—being sentimentalized and put on a pedestal. As such, it is important not to venerate the "quiet, weak, perpetual virgin," but instead the "awesome, powerful, beautiful, and fertile Queen of Heaven."[66]

---

[61] See Kittredge Cherry, *Art That Dares: Gay Jesus, Woman Christ, and More* (Berkeley, CA: Androgyne Press, 2007), 73.

[62] Leo Steinberg, *The Sexuality of Christ in Renaissance Art and in Modern Oblivion*, 2nd ed. (Chicago: University of Chicago Press, 1996).

[63] See, e.g., Cornwall, "Apophasis and Ambiguity"; Cornwall, "The *Kenosis* of Unambiguous Sex in the Body of Christ"; Gross, "Intersexuality and Scripture."

[64] See Susan Stryker, *Transgender History* (Berkeley, CA: Seal Press, 2008), 138–39. It is estimated that one out of every 200 children is born with some sort of "intersex matrix." See Mollenkott, *Omnigender*, 45.

[65] McNeill, *Taking a Chance on God*, 138.

[66] Williams, *Just as I Am*, 110.

Finally, Mary dissolves gender boundaries through the ways in which she has been portrayed in the popular imagination. For example, Elizabeth Stuart has shown that, prior to the twentieth century, Mary was often depicted as a "Virgin Priest," which "defies the sexual conventions" of those periods during which only men could receive holy orders. Indeed, Mary has been depicted in art as wearing the vestments of a priest or even the *pallium* of a bishop.[67] Similarly, Marcella Althaus-Reid cites the Latin American tradition of Santa Librada, who is depicted as a sexually ambiguous young woman who is crucified in the same way as Jesus Christ. For Althaus-Reid, this is an example of a transgender Mary—a "popular ambiguous divine cross-dresser of the poor."[68] Thus, both the Virgin Priest and Santa Librada are examples of how Mary has erased gender boundaries in the popular imagination.

It seems appropriate to close this section with Gerard Loughlin's concluding words to his introductory essay to *Queer Theology*. Loughlin notes how truly queer Mary is:

> *Mary with her crying infant is a perfect figure for queer theology. She is a virgin who yet gives birth; a mother for whom there is no father other than the one she comes to see in her son. And her son, when grown into the Christ of faith and heart, in turn gives birth to her, to the ecclesia he feeds, with his blood as once he was fed with her milk. And then this son takes her—his mother and child—as his bride and queen, so that we can hardly say who comes from whom, who lives in whom, or how we have come to find our own bodies remade in Christ's: fed with his flesh which is also Mary's.*[69]

---

[67] Stuart, "Priest at the Altar," 134.
[68] Althaus-Reid, *Indecent Theology*, 80.
[69] Loughlin, "Introduction," 32.

Study Questions

1. What role does Mary play in your own spiritual life and development? How do you understand Mary as the bearer of radical love?

2. How has mariology been an oppressive doctrine for women, especially in the context of Latin American liberation theologies?

3. Why can LGBT people be viewed as Mary's "special children"? How else does Mary challenge family boundaries?

4. What does it mean to describe Mary as the "marker of the irrational"?

5. How might Mary challenge gender boundaries as well as the development of intersex theology?

For Further Study

Mary
- Althaus-Reid, *Indecent Theology*, 45–86 ("The Indecent Virgin").
- Beattie, "Queen of Heaven."
- Loughlin, "Introduction," 31–32 ("Queer *Mixtio*").
- McNeill, *Taking a Chance on God*, 137–43 ("The Relationship between Mary, the Mother of God, and the Gay and Lesbian Community").
- Stuart, "Priest at the Altar," 132–34.
- Ward, "Displaced Body," 164–65 ("Incarnation and Circumcision").

Atonement: Ending Scapegoating through Radical Love

What is the significance of Jesus Christ's life, death, and resurrection for us? How has Jesus Christ reconciled us—or made us "at-one"—with God? That is the central question addressed by the doctrine of atonement. This section proposes that the doctrine of atonement can be understood as *ending scapegoating through radical love*. In other words, Jesus Christ's death can be understood as the end of endless divisions between "insiders" and "outsiders." That is, through the crucifixion, God has revealed and declared a resounding "No!" to the scapegoating mechanism through which the "insiders" within society target and eliminate those who are innocent "outsiders."

Queer Scapegoats

Many LGBT people were scapegoated by our peers growing up because we did not fit within the typical gender norms. For example, I felt more comfortable in elementary school reading books, jumping rope, and playing four square with the girls in my class instead of kickball with the other boys. Indeed, some of us may have been bullied by classmates in school not because we did anything wrong, but rather because we were perceived as being different or "outsiders."[70] This dynamic is illustrated vividly in William Golding's *Lord of the Flies*, in which a group of boys stranded on a deserted island ends up targeting and killing one of their classmates named Piggy who was perceived to be weak and an "outsider." The issue of anti-LGBT bullying and scapegoating has taken on a particular urgency in light of the horrific string of suicides in the United States in the fall of 2010 of young men (some as young as thirteen) who were tormented by their classmates because they were—or were perceived to be—gay.[71]

---

[70] For a discussion of "insiders" and "outsiders" in the Bible, see Lawrence M. Wills, *Not God's People: Insiders and Outsiders in the Biblical World* (Lanham, MD: Rowman and Littlefield, 2008). For a helpful listing of different kinds of "outsiders" and oppressions in our society, see William M. Kondrath, *God's Tapestry: Understanding and Celebrating Differences* (Herndon, VA: Alban Institute, 2008), 45.

[71] See Patrick S. Cheng, "Faith, Hope and Love: Ending LGBT Teen Suicide," *Huffington Post* (Oct. 6, 2010), http://www.huffingtonpost.com/rev-patrick-s-cheng-phd/faith-hope-and-love-endin_b_749160.html. For some of the struggles of gay and lesbian students in Catholic high schools, see Michael Maher, *Being Gay and Lesbian in a Catholic High School: Beyond the Uniform* (Binghamton, NY: Harrington Park Press, 2001).

The literary theorist René Girard has written extensively about the scapegoating mechanism and its relationship to Jesus Christ. For Girard, society consists of competing factions that could erupt into violence at any time. Girard argues, however, that this suppressed violence is often channeled toward a scapegoat, that is, an innocent and helpless victim who is usually marked by difference. Once the scapegoat is expelled or destroyed, societal order is restored. This mechanism then repeats itself over and over again.[72]

According to Girard, the significance of Jesus Christ's life, death, and resurrection is that it is an unveiling—and rejection—of this system of scapegoating. As the ultimate scapegoat (that is, as the sacrificial victim *par excellence*), Jesus Christ condemns and puts to an end the need to scapegoat others. For Girard, Jesus Christ is the ultimate scapegoat, and the resurrection represents God's emphatic rejection—or "No!"—to this dynamic of "insiders" vs. "outsiders."

In many ways, queer people today can be seen as scapegoats of the larger society. In other words, society often channels its repressed violence—either metaphorically or literally—toward LGBT people, who are seen as different or as "outsiders" as a result of our marginalized sexualities and/or gender identities. As such, we are often the target of discrimination, and sometimes even violence, for the sake of preserving order in society.

Ending the Cycle of Violence

Chris Glaser has discussed what atonement means to him as an openly gay theologian. Glaser reinterprets traditional atonement theology (that is, Jesus Christ died for our sins) in terms of René Girard's scapegoating theory. For Glaser, queer people often serve as the scapegoats for non-queer people in the church who are wrestling with the shame and alienation of their own bodies or their own sexual sins. Rather than face these difficult issues themselves, these non-queer people seek to channel their self-loathing and negativity upon the scapegoat.

---

[72] See Glaser, *Coming Out as Sacrament*, 20–24; see also Lev. 16:7–10.

As a result, LGBT people become the scapegoats for our society, and we pay a price for being different, whether it is being forced to live in the closet, denied ordination, or excluded from church leadership roles.[73] Glaser believes that God is present at Jesus Christ's crucifixion, but that God does not demand Jesus' death as a sacrifice for humanity's sins. Rather, God is present at the crucifixion because God desires to heal the breach and stop the repeated cycle of violence against scapegoats.[74]

Multiple Substitutions

James Alison has also written about the doctrine of the atonement, which, like Glaser's discussion, centers around the Girardian notion of a scapegoat. For Alison, however, the significance of Jesus Christ's death is that he substitutes himself for a "series of substitutions."[75] In other words, even though animal sacrifices previously had replaced the primitive practice of human sacrifice, Jesus now takes the place of the animal as the High Priest and the Lamb of God. By substituting himself for humanity at the moment of sacrifice, Jesus unmasks the dynamics of what is really going on. That is, Jesus reveals to the world the cruelty of the sacrificial system.[76]

Taking Alison's notion of substitution one step further, we see how atonement is a queer doctrine indeed. That is, if Jesus Christ takes the place of humanity as the ultimate sacrifice, then his body becomes a site of multiple sexualities and gender identities. As such, Jesus Christ becomes a multisexed and multigendered body through this substitution, just as the body of Christ (as the church) is itself made up of multiple sexes and genders. As Mark Jordan points out, "In much Christian doctrine, the central claim of vicarious atonement requires multiple exchanges of identity. The Lord's sacrifice on the cross can be applied for salvation only by a sort of substitution of persons, without regard for their sexes or genders. Christianity

---

[73] See Glaser, *Coming Out as Sacrament*, 33.

[74] See Glaser, *Coming Out as Sacrament*, 39

[75] James Alison, *Undergoing God: Dispatches from the Scene of a Break-In* (New York: Continuum, 2006), 58.

[76] For a theological and political reflection on what can be gained by representations of violence and pain, see Kent L. Brintnall, *Ecce Homo: The Male-Body-in-Pain as Redemptive Figure* (Chicago: University of Chicago Press, 2011) (forthcoming).

is a religion of exchanging identities without sex."[77] Thus, the doctrine of atonement not only erases the boundaries between "insiders" and "outsiders," but it also dissolves the boundaries of sexuality and gender.

Of course, not everyone subscribes to this sacrificial model of atonement. Some people, for example, prefer the moral influence theory of atonement that was proposed by the eleventh-century theologian Peter Abelard. According to that theory, Jesus' death is salvific in that it results in a subjective change, or repentance, within those of us who hear about this death. For those who prefer this moral influence theory of atonement, Jesus Christ's life, death, and resurrection still can be understood as radical love. Specifically, the crucifixion is an act of radical love by God because it causes us to rethink and to repent of our own biases against those who have different sexualities and gender identities. It dissolves the binary of "us" vs. "them" as the result of our *metanoia* or repentance.

In sum, for many LGBT people, the doctrine of the atonement can be understood as the end of scapegoating through radical love. This act of radical love is so extreme that it results in the dissolving of boundaries between "insiders" and "outsiders." In a sermon that was preached at a memorial service for Matthew Shepard—the young gay man who was brutally beaten and left to die on a fence near Laramie, Wyoming—the Reverend Thomas Troeger proclaimed that Christ's "full, perfect and sufficient sacrifice" means that there are:

> *No more scapegoats*
> *No more chanting:*
> *"You're out, you're out,*
> *you can't come in!"*[78]

---

[77] Mark D. Jordan, "Sodomites and Churchmen: The Theological Invention of Homosexuality," in Bernauer and Carrette, *Michel Foucault and Theology*, 240.

[78] Thomas H. Troeger, "No More Scapegoats," in Hinnant, *God Comes Out*, 46.

Study Questions

1. How can atonement be understood as the ending of scapegoating through radical love?

2. Have you ever been bullied or scapegoated as an "outsider"? Have you ever bullied or scapegoated others as an "insider"?

3. Describe the Girardian view of the scapegoating mechanism and also the role that Jesus Christ plays in that framework.

4. How are LGBT people often scapegoats of the larger society?

5. How does Jesus Christ's substitution of himself in the place of humanity result in a multisexed and multigendered body of Christ?

6. What is your view of the substitutionary atonement theory? The moral influence atonement theory?

For Further Study

Atonement
- Alison, *Undergoing God*, 50–67 ("An Atonement Update").
- Glaser, *Coming Out as Sacrament*, 17–34 ("Sacrifices and Scapegoats").
- Troeger, "No More Scapegoats."

Chapter Five

Holy Spirit: The Return to Radical Love

Having first discussed God as the sending forth of radical love, and then Jesus Christ as the recovery of radical love, we now turn to the doctrine of the Holy Spirit, the third person of the Trinity. The Holy Spirit is often marginalized in Western Christianity, which tends to focus on the relationship between the first and second persons of Trinity (that is, God and Jesus Christ). It is no surprise, therefore, that pneumatology, or the study of the Holy Spirit, is an underdeveloped subject in queer theology. So it seems appropriate for a book on queer theology to close by focusing on the member of the Trinity that occupies a marginalized position in theological discourse.

Who is the Holy Spirit for LGBT people today? The theme of this chapter is that the Holy Spirit is all about the *return to radical love*. That is, the Holy Spirit continues along the trajectory that first started with God sending forth radical love and second with Jesus Christ recovering the radical love that had been rejected by humanity. We can understand this third and final movement as the Holy Spirit *helping* us to return to the radical love from which we all came. It makes sense for us to understand the Holy Spirit's role as a helper, since one of its biblical names is "paraclete" or "*paraklētos*," which can be translated as "advocate" or "helper."[1]

As we have seen previously, radical love is defined as a love so extreme that it dissolves all kinds of boundaries. Indeed, the thesis of this book is that both the queer experience and Christian theology are fundamentally about radical love. In this chapter, we will see how various boundaries are dissolved repeatedly, not only in the context of the Holy Spirit itself, but also in the related doctrines of the church, the saints, the

---

[1] During the Last Supper, Jesus tells his disciples that God will give them another *paraklēton*—or "Advocate"—who will be with them forever. See John 14:16.

sacraments, and, finally, last things. All of these doctrines share the same goal, or *telos*, which is our return to the radical love from which we first came.

Indeed, our ultimate return to radical love can be understood as sanctification. That is, sanctification is all about our eventual reunion with God (and all creation) so that the barriers that separate us from God (and from creation) are dissolved. This is the restoration of all things, or *apokatastasis*, as described by the great second-century theologian Origen. Each of us may require some purification by fire—in the same way that precious metals are refined—before we get there, but ultimately we *will* get there with the help of the Holy Spirit.

Holy Spirit: Pointing Us toward Radical Love

As an Eagle Scout and former camp counselor, I like to think about the Holy Spirit as an old-fashioned magnetic compass. Alternatively, for those who are more high-tech, the Holy Spirit can be thought of as a GPS (global positioning system) device that we use in our cars to help guide us on our journey. In other words, the Holy Spirit is a helper in that it always leads us to our final destination, which I have described as the return to radical love, or the dissolving of all boundaries that divide us from God and neighbor. It is in this sense (that is, as a helper) that the Holy Spirit can be understood in traditional terms as the "giver of life" who has "spoken through the prophets."

Holy Spirit as Gaydar

Many LGBT people joke about having "gaydar," or the ability to sense who else in the room is queer simply by reading the subtle unspoken "signals" that said queer people transmit (which, by the way, supports the view of sexuality and gender identity as performance). In a way, the Holy Spirit is like gaydar; it helps direct us to radical love, whether divine or human. As Sarah Coakley, the Cambridge University theologian, has noted, there is an fundamental connection between the desire for God in deep prayer and the desire for another person in sexual passion. Indeed, Coakley argues that "in any prayer of the sort in which we radically cede control to the Spirit there is an instant reminder of the close analogue between this ceding (to the trinitarian God), and the *ekstasis* of human sexual passion."[2]

This fundamental connection between the Holy Spirit, the desire for God, and sexual passion is illustrated by a humorous story that Robert Williams tells about his friend, another openly gay minister, who, at the moment of a particularly intense orgasm during an anonymous sexual encounter on a beach, started inexplicably to engage in glossolalia, or the charismatic practice of speaking in tongues (which, in charismatic circles is understood as signifying the presence of the Holy Spirit). As Williams' friend explained, "No longer could I differentiate between the sexual experience and my prayer life. In the spirit, I prayed. In a new language of ecstasy, I spoke. Some call it tongues, others the language of private prayer. I knew it to be a private communication between God and me."[3] Indeed, who hasn't invoked—or heard—the divine name during a particularly intense orgasm or sexual experience?

The Holy Spirit is not just about sexual passion, however. It is also the one who guides us in unexpected ways to falling in love with others. Falling in love is an odd thing; it is not usually something that one can plan in advance or force upon the other party. As such, the Holy Spirit can be viewed as a kind of queer "super glue" that dissolves the normal boundaries that separate people and bonds together the persons who are brought together in radical love.

Holy Spirit as Dissolver of Boundaries

The Holy Spirit also serves to guide us to radical love by dissolving various boundaries that we normally think of as fixed or impermeable. One such boundary is the dividing line between *sexuality vs. church*. Most people think of these two categories as mutually exclusive; in general, one does not talk about sexuality and church in the same breath. However, this very boundary was dissolved through the guidance of the

---

[2] Sarah Coakley, "Living into the Mystery of the Holy Trinity: Trinity, Prayer, and Sexuality," in *The Holy Spirit: Classic and Contemporary Readings*, ed. Eugene F. Rogers (Malden, MA: Wiley-Blackwell, 2009), 45.

[3] Williams, *Just as I Am*, 204.

Holy Spirit in the founding of the Metropolitan Community Churches (MCC)—the worldwide denomination founded by and for LGBT people but open to all—by Troy Perry in 1968. Perry, the Pentecostal minister who had been kicked out of his denomination for being gay, recounts praying to God and asking for the Holy Spirit to show him a church that would be for all outcasts. In that moment, Perry was inspired to found MCC in the living room of his home in Los Angeles.

A second boundary dissolved by the Holy Spirit is the dividing line between *private vs. public* discourse about one's sexuality. Again, for most people these categories are mutually exclusive; in general, discussions of non-normative sexualities and practices are limited to the private sphere. However, James Alison, the openly gay Catholic theologian, explains how the Holy Spirit collapses this distinction between private and public whenever people come out of the closet. According to Alison, the gift of the Holy Spirit occupies the private places of shame and toxicity with such gentleness that we are able to let go of such feelings internally. The Holy Spirit allows us to move in accordance with what God has called us to do; the Holy Spirit collapses our closets and frees us to come out.[4] Another example of this dynamic of collapsing the private and the public occurred at the Stonewall Riots of 1969, which is considered to be the founding event of the modern LGBT-rights movement. According to Robert Williams, "the Holy Spirit was at work among the drag queens and bulldykes in the Stonewall Inn that evening" and empowered them to fight back publicly against the police that frequently raided the secretive culture of gay bars.[5]

A third boundary dissolved by the Holy Spirit is the line between *unity vs. diversity*. For Thomas Bohache, the openly gay theologian and ordained minister in the Metropolitan Community Churches, the significance of the very first Pentecost —when the Holy Spirit descended upon the apostles in tongues of fire—is how the apostles were all gathered in one place, yet the Holy Spirit manifested itself within them in different ways.

---

[4] Alison, *Undergoing God*, 208–13.
[5] Williams, *Just as I Am*, 189.

As a result, all of the onlookers were able to hear the gospel in their own language. Thus, God's message was shared in "many different ways according to the hearer's individual needs."[6]

For Bohache, the significance of the Pentecost story is that LGBT people are called by the Holy Spirit to resist the heteronormative patterns of relationships. That is, the diversity of the LGBT community is to be celebrated—whether it is gay senior citizens, queer young people, the BDSM leather community,[7] or the drag community—in whatever space they find themselves, whether it is a "bar, bathhouse, women's spaces, 12-Step group, synagogue, church, mosque, ashram, sex club, rodeo, book group, coffee house, university or seminary classroom."[8] According to Bohache, the queer movement is a "new Pentecost" that allows the Holy Spirit to "blow where it chooses" and "opens the doors and windows wide, blows out negativity, despair and inhospitality."[9]

A fourth and final boundary that is dissolved by the Holy Spirit is the line between *law vs. lawlessness*. Eugene Rogers, an openly gay theologian at the University of North Carolina Greensboro, demonstrates that the Holy Spirit operates both by law and by freedom. Rogers argues that marriage—whether same-sex or opposite-sex—is "ruled" by the Holy Spirit, whose work can described as *faithfulness* (that is, it is the Holy Spirit who expresses the faithfulness of God in raising Jesus Christ from the dead). For those who would argue that being "ruled" by the Holy Spirit is essentially a license to lawlessness (that is, antinomian behavior), Rogers responds by noting that the Holy Spirit actually operates in accordance with a rule—the "Rule of faith-keeping"—and thus is *not* antinomian in nature.[10] As such,

---

[6] Thomas Bohache, "Pentecost Queered," in Guest et al., *Queer Bible Commentary*, 568.

[7] As noted above, for many LGBT people the practices of bondage, discipline, and sadomasochism (BDSM) can be a deeply spiritual experience. See, e.g., Dossie Easton and Janet W. Hardy, *Radical Ecstasy: SM Journeys to Transcendence* (Oakland, CA: Greenery Press, 2004); Peterson, "Gay Men's Spiritual Experience in the Leather Community"; Jack Rinella, *Philosophy in the Dungeon: The Magic of Sex and Spirit* (Chicago: Rinella Editorial Services, 2006). Although BDSM may appear to the uninitiated as being about domination and exploitation, it is actually a highly mutual practice in which the ethical norms of "safe, sane, and consensual" apply. That is, all scenes are highly negotiated between the participating parties as equals, and the bottom can terminate the scene at any time by the use of a safe word.

[8] Bohache, "Pentecost Queered," 568.

[9] Bohache, "Pentecost Queered," 570.

[10] Indeed, as noted above, the principle of radical love itself is not a license to lawlessness. It is fundamentally about love, and, at a minimum, the ethical norms of "safe, sane, and consensual" apply.

the Holy Spirit dissolves the artificial boundary between law vs. lawlessness in that it manifests itself in both fidelity and freedom."[11]

As a student once said to me, the Holy Spirit is the queerest of the three persons of the Trinity. It operates across time and space. It is fluid and difficult to nail down (even in its physical manifestation as a dove or tongues of fire). And yet, the Holy Spirit is our helper, or paraclete, that returns us to the radical love that was originally sent by God, lost by humanity, and recovered by Jesus Christ. Indeed, the Holy Spirit works in unexpected and surprising ways.

Study Questions

1. Who do you understand the Holy Spirit to be? How has the Holy Spirit worked in your life?

2. How is the Holy Spirit like a queer compass or GPS system? How does the Holy Spirit point us to radical love?

3. What do you think about characterizing the work of the Holy Spirit as gaydar?

4. What are some connections between glossolalia (speaking in tongues) and ecstasy?

5. What are some ways in which the Holy Spirit dissolves boundaries that we normally think of as being fixed or impermeable, such as the boundaries between sexuality and the church, private and public discourse about sexuality, unity and diversity, and law and lawlessness?

For Further Study

Holy Spirit
* Alison, "Place of Shame and the Giving of the Spirit."
* Bohache, "Pentecost Queered."
* Coakley, "Living into the Mystery of the Holy Trinity."
* Rogers, "Shape of the Body and the Shape of Grace."

---

[11] Rogers, *Sexuality and the Christian Body*, 247–48.

Church: External Community of Radical Love

For the earliest Christians, coming together as a community was an act of subversion. It was the creation of a radically new "family" or "body" that transcended biological relationships and the established social order. It was a rehearsal for the end times, when the human body, with its physical attributes, would be raised as a spiritual body, or *pneumatikos sōma*.[12] In other words, church was an *external community of radical love*. That is, the church was a new community that dissolved traditional boundaries that kept people apart such as biological relationships, social class, and physical attributes.

In some ways, the families of choice that queer people have created (such as same-sex and gender-variant marriages, domestic partnerships, polyamorous relationships, and broader friendship networks) can be viewed as communities of radical love. Like the early church, these communities are new "families" and "bodies" that cut across traditional boundaries that separate us. Indeed, the rainbow flag and annual pride marches are symbolic of this ideal for the LGBT community. These symbols mark us as a community that aspires to dissolve boundaries based on traditional identity markers.

Indeed, to the extent that the church is one body that is made up of people of many sexualities, genders, and races, we can understand the church as a place that dissolves the traditional boundaries that divide us from one another. As Galatians reminds us, there is neither male nor female in Christ Jesus.[13] This gathering up of God's people, regardless of sexuality, gender identity, and other differences, is the work of the Holy Spirit and is a way of returning us to the radical love that was sent by the first person of the Trinity, and the radical love that was recovered by the second person of the Trinity.

As someone who has worked for the Episcopal Church for more than a decade—first as a lawyer for one of its official agencies and now as a professor at the Episcopal Divinity School—I have admired the ways in which this denomination is

---

[12] 1 Cor. 15:44.
[13] Gal. 3:28.

fundamentally "queer" to the extent that it dissolves the boundaries between Roman Catholicism and Protestantism. Formed
out of the Elizabethan Settlement, the Anglican Communion has
always tried to preserve the best of both traditions, whether it is
the rich sacramental liturgical tradition of Roman Catholicism
or the reformed theology of Protestantism.[14] Although the
Anglican Communion is currently being challenged globally
over LGBT issues,[15] my deepest hope is that its unique history
of boundary-crossing will allow it to flourish and thrive.

Four Marks of the Church

Traditionally speaking, ecclesiology—that is, the doctrine of
the church—has focused on the four marks of the church as
expressed in the Nicene Creed: one, holy, catholic, and apos-
tolic. In this section, we will cover each of these four marks in
the context of the queer experience and specifically how these
marks each dissolve the traditional boundaries that separate us.

Oneness The first classical mark of the church is oneness. In
terms of this mark, Elizabeth Stuart points out the paradox that
a community truly marked by oneness would actually recognize a variety of relational configurations between its members
and *not* just marriage and singleness. For Stuart, Christians
are called to a state of "permanent porousness" in terms of
opening ourselves to others. One way of opening ourselves to
others, for example, is through marriage and sexual relationships. However, all too often a sexual relationship (for example,
a married couple) becomes an entity unto itself and withdraws
from the larger body of Christ. Therefore, Stuart believes that
we are actually called into all kinds of relationships—such
as friendship—within the larger body of Christ. This kind of
radical love described by Stuart—that is, dissolving the rigid
line between marriage and singleness—would actually serve to
strengthen the "oneness" of the church.[16]

---

[14] See, e.g., Ian T. Douglas, "The Exigency of Times and Occasions: Power and Identity in the Anglican Communion
Today," in *Beyond Colonial Anglicanism: The Anglican Communion in the Twenty-First Century*, ed. Ian T. Douglas and
Kwok Pui-lan (New York: Church Publishing, 2001), 35–39.
[15] See Brown, *Other Voices, Other Worlds*.
[16] Stuart, *Gay and Lesbian Theologies*, 113.

Similarly, Paul Lakeland, a professor of Catholic studies at Fairfield University, has proposed a new "ecclesiology of desire" in order to encourage a greater oneness within the church. Specifically, Lakeland argues that the church should stop using the metaphor of heterosexual marriage to describe itself (for example, describing the church as the bride of Christ). For Lakeland, the notion of a spouse implies a degree of possession and permanence in relationships that is inconsistent with the characteristics of relational "porousness" as described by Stuart. Instead, Lakeland argues that the church should use *desire* as a metaphor to describe itself.[17] A focus on desire—that is, a longing for an ever-closer relationship with others—opens up a myriad of queer relational configurations, from platonic friendships to one-night stands to life partners, and thus ultimately strengthens the oneness of the ecclesial community.

Holiness The second mark of the church is holiness. Stuart describes this as where the divine meets the human, or where God's grace is manifested on earth. For Stuart, the holy occurs whenever we attempt to give back to God what God has done for us. Specifically, what God has done for us is characterized by the sheer gift of grace, which can only be "repaid" in our own radical generosity and hospitality to others. Thus, a community marked by holiness is one that exhibits radical generosity and hospitality to others.[18]

Kathy Rudy has written about how anonymous sexual encounters actually can be a form of hospitality and welcome to others. What Rudy proposes is an ethic of hospitality, which is essentially the reversal of the Sodom and Gomorrah narrative. Indeed, the early Christian church was marked by its generosity of welcoming those who were outsiders. As such, this ethic of hospitality should be the overriding norm for all issues, including sexuality. As a result, certain sexual acts—including anonymous or communal sex—would not be forbidden *per se*, but rather measured by the degree to which the actions are welcoming or hospitable.

---

[17] See Paul Lakeland, "Ecclesiology, Desire, and the Erotic," in Kamitsuka, *The Embrace of Eros*.
[18] See Stuart, *Gay and Lesbian Theologies*, 113.

As a result of this ethic, according to Rudy, "all genders are collapsed into Christian, and all Christians go about the seamless work of God." The only distinction that ultimately matters is whether one is "working toward the new creation" (that is, "church") or not (that is, the "world").[19] Thus, extrapolating from Rudy's ethic of hospitality, queer people—indeed, all people—might very well find ecclesial holiness in a variety of unorthodox places, including a circuit party,[20] a gathering for nude erotic massage at the Body Electric School,[21] or a sex party. This, indeed, would be a manifestation of church as radical love.

Catholicity The third mark of the church is catholicity. Stuart describes this as unity in difference. That is, the church catholic is "firmly centered but nevertheless dynamic and spilling out in difference."[22] This catholicity arises out of the fact that there is only one body of Christ, but it is nevertheless made up of all believers, which include a multiplicity of gender identities, sexes, sexualities, races, cultures, ages, and abilities. To the extent that the church is literally the body of Christ, then the church itself is also one and many.

Ironically, it is the Roman Catholic Church that has failed to recognize this "catholic" unity in difference with respect to issues relating to sexuality and gender identities. Mark Jordan argues that it is the very silences and denials of queerness by the Roman Catholic Church leadership that allows an entire subculture of camp to exist within the priesthood. According to Jordan, traits that would be otherwise "stigmatized in men"— such as "effeminacy, artifice, 'aestheticism'" as well as "fervent religious worship"—are not only permitted but encouraged in the Catholic priesthood. Such actions become "camp" precisely because the church loudly insists that there is "absolutely

---

[19] Rudy, *Sex and the Church*, 129.
[20] See, e.g., Wil Rombotis Brant, "Why Go to Church When You Can Drink with Mary?: Gaymale Clubculture as Religion Without Religion Against Ethics," *Theology and Sexuality*, no. 15 (Sept. 2001): 32–44; Paul J. Gorrell, "Rite to Party: Circuit Parties and Religious Experience," in Thumma and Gray, *Gay Religion*, 313–26.
[21] See, e.g., Goss, *Queering Christ*, 56–71 ("Finding God in the Heart-Genital Connection"); Michael Bernard Kelly, *Seduced by Grace: Contemporary Spirituality, Gay Experience, and Christian Faith* (Melbourne, Australia: Clouds of Magellan, 2007), 211–14 (discussing rimming and anal pleasure).
[22] Stuart, *Gay and Lesbian Theologies*, 114.

nothing queer" about them.[23] Jordan cites the queer theorist Eve Sedgwick in noting how Roman Catholicism creates a space that affirms a lifestyle of unmarried adults, "men in dresses," theater, and fetish.[24]

Indeed, it is often in the context of queer churches—such as the Metropolitan Community Churches and The Fellowship—that unity in difference is honored. Not only are these churches welcoming of people of diverse backgrounds, including diverse sexualities and gender identities (as well as queer-identified allies), but these churches also provide a space in which people can engage in diverse forms of prayer, worship, and liturgy[25] as well as a wide variety of justice-seeking ministries, including operating food pantries and homeless shelters, providing HIV/AIDS care, seeking marriage equality, countering ex-gay movements, and opposing violence against queer people around the world. This is what true catholicity is all about.

Apostolicity The fourth and final mark of the church is apostolicity. Stuart describes this as signifying an institution that "stands in a dynamic tradition and in a communion of saints." As such, Stuart understands the church as needing to exhibit both a "positive and deep engagement with the Christian tradition" and a humility that is "manifest in a willingness to consider the possibility that we might be wrong."[26]

Apostolicity is also derived from the Greek word *apostolos*, or that which is sent forth. As such, mission—or the sending forth of the gospel—takes on particular importance in terms of the increasing importance of cyberspace and technological advances in the queer community. Through such advances, queer people are able to form virtual ecclesial communities with other like-minded people, regardless of how much we might

[23] Mark D. Jordan, *The Silence of Sodom: Homosexuality in Modern Catholicism* (Chicago: University of Chicago Press, 2000), 186.
[24] Jordan, *Silence of Sodom*, 187.
[25] See, e.g., Kittredge Cherry and Zalmon Sherwood, eds., *Equal Rites: Lesbian and Gay Worship, Ceremonies, and Celebrations* (Louisville, KY: Westminster John Knox Press, 1995); Geoffrey Duncan, *Courage to Love: Liturgies for the Lesbian, Gay, Bisexual, and Transgender Community* (Cleveland, OH: Pilgrim Press, 2002); Siobhan Garrigan, "Queer Worship," *Theology and Sexuality* 15. no. 2 (May 2009): 211–30; Chris Glaser, *Coming Out to God: Prayers for Lesbians and Gay Men, Their Families and Friends* (Louisville, KY: Westminster John Knox Press, 1991); William G. Storey, *Book of Prayer for Gay and Lesbian Christians* (New York: Crossroad Publishing, 2002); Stuart, "Making No Sense," 113–23.
[26] Stuart, *Gay and Lesbian Theologies*, 114.

be isolated with respect to physical geography. Indeed, the Internet allows for God's radical love to permeate throughout the world in "real time." Kate O'Riordan and Heather White have written about the increasing phenomenon of online queer spiritual practices, including churches in Second Life, which is a virtual 3-D world.[27]

Whether it is on a social network, a hook-up site, or a chatroom, queer people increasingly connect around the world and practice radical love in community.[28] In the fluid world of cyberspace, linguistic divisions as well as other boundaries—such as sexuality, gender, class, and geography—dissolve before our very eyes. This has been the case, for example, with the Queer Asian Spirit website and listserv, which has, since 2000, brought together LGBT Asian persons of faith from all around the world.[29] These issues about apostolicity in the digital world all raise important questions about the mission of the church in breaking down boundaries of physical space and cyberspace.[30]

Queer Pastoral Care

A second important cluster of issues relating to ecclesiology is that of pastoral care. It is through the church—an external community of radical love—that LGBT people can minister to each other and find spiritual, emotional, and physical healing in community. As with other marginalized groups, LGBT people have unique pastoral needs. This was particularly the case in the 1980s and 1990s, when the gay male community was decimated by HIV/AIDS.[31] Although the HIV/AIDS crisis continues today—and particularly within the two-thirds world—the advent of protease inhibitors has markedly prolonged the

---

[27] Kate O'Riordan and Heather White, "Virtual Believers: Queer Spiritual Practice Online," in *Queer Spiritual Spaces: Sexuality and Sacred Places*, ed. Kath Browne, Sally R. Munt, and Andrew K.T. Yip (Farnham, UK: Ashgate, 2010), 199–230.

[28] See Stefanie Knauss, "Transcendental Relationships?: A Theological Reflection on Cybersex and Cyber-Relationships," *Theology and Sexuality* 15, no. 3 (Sept. 2009): 329–48; see also Julie Lytle, "Virtual Incarnations: Exploration of Internet-Mediated Interaction as Manifestations of the Divine," *Religious Education* 105, no. 4 (July 2010): 395–412.

[29] See Cheng, "Reclaiming Our Traditions, Rituals, and Spaces," 238. The Queer Asian Spirit website can be found at http://www.queerasianspirit.org.

[30] For a theology of a mission-shaped church, see Christopher Duraisingh, "From Church-Shaped Mission to Mission-Shaped Church," *Anglican Theological Review* 92, no. 2 (Winter 2010): 7–28.

[31] See Fortunato, *AIDS, The Spiritual Dilemma*; Hardy, *Loving Men*; William D. Lindsey, "The AIDS Crisis and the Church: A Time to Heal," *Theology and Sexuality*, no. 2 (March 1995): 11–37; Ronald E. Long and J. Michael Clark, *AIDS, God, and Faith* (Las Colinas, TX: Monument Press, 1992).

lifespan of people living with HIV/AIDS.[32] Nevertheless, there still are difficult issues that face the gay male community today, including the increasing rate of HIV/AIDS infection as a result of the practice of barebacking (that is, unprotected anal sex).[33]

In recent years, a number of helpful resources on pastoral care issues for LGBT people have been published, including *Ministry Among God's Queer Folk: LGBT Pastoral Care.*[34] Other books on the topic of LGBT pastoral care include: *Counseling Lesbian Partners*; *Discovering Images of God: Narratives of Care Among Lesbians and Gay Men*; *Spiritual Direction and the Gay Person* (1998); *Pastoral Care of Gays, Lesbians, and Their Families*; and *Passing Through: The End-of-Life Decisions of Lesbians and Gay Men.*[35] Recently the Metropolitan Community Churches published a resource guide, *TRANSformative Church Ministry Program*, for parishes that want to create a welcome space for transgender and gender-variant people.[36] Pastoral care is ultimately an issue of radical love because it is a love that is so powerful that it dissolves the boundaries between isolation and community. Through church communities and pastoral care, LGBT people are brought out of isolation and into an external community of radical love.

---

[32] For a resource guide relating to people affected by HIV/AIDS, see Joshua L. Love and Metropolitan Community Church Global HIV/AIDS Ministry, *Uncommon Hope: A DVD Enhanced Curriculum Reflection the Heart of the Church for People Affected by HIV/AIDS* (Victoria, Canada: Trafford Publishing, 2009).

[33] See Goss, *Queering Christ*, 72–87 (discussing ethical and spiritual dimensions to barebacking).

[34] David J. Kundtz and Bernard S. Schlager, *Ministry Among God's Queer Folk: LGBT Pastoral Care* (Cleveland, OH: Pilgrim Press, 2007).

[35] Joretta L. Marshall, *Counseling Lesbian Partners* (Louisville, KY: Westminster John Knox Press, 1997); Larry Kent Graham, *Discovering Images of God: Narratives of Care Among Lesbians and Gay Men* (Louisville, KY: Westminster John Knox Press, 1997); James L. Empereur, *Spiritual Direction and the Gay Person* (New York: Continuum, 1998); David K. Switzer, *Pastoral Care of Gays, Lesbians, and Their Families* (Minneapolis, MN: Fortress Press, 1999); Jeanette A. Auger, *Passing Through: The End-of-Life Decisions of Lesbians and Gay Men* (Halifax, Canada: Fernwood Publishing, 2003).

[36] Metropolitan Community Churches, *TRANSformative Church Ministry Program* (October 4, 2010).

Study Questions

1. How is the church understood to be an external community of radical love? What was your experience of church growing up, and what is your relationship to the institutional church today?

2. How does "permanent porousness," or the ongoing longing for deeper relationships with others, relate to the oneness of the church?

3. How might sexual hospitality be a mark of holiness of the church? In what ways can you imagine being hospitable to others, sexually or otherwise?

4. How does catholicity relate to unity and diversity in the LGBT community? What kinds of diverse church communities have you experienced?

5. How does cyberspace relate to the apostolicity of the church? Where have you found church in cyberspace?

6. What does it mean to define pastoral care as the dissolution of the boundary between isolation and community for LGBT people?

For Further Study

Church

Oneness
- Lakeland, "Ecclesiology, Desire, and the Erotic."

Holiness
- Rudy, *Sex and the Church.*

Catholicity
- Jordan, *Silence of Sodom.*
- Jordan, *Telling Truths in Church.*

Apostolicity
- Cheng, "Reclaiming Our Traditions, Rituals, and Spaces."
- O'Riordan and White, "Virtual Believers."

Worship and Liturgy
- Cherry and Sherwood, *Equal Rites.*
- Duncan, *Courage to Love.*
- Garrigan, "Queer Worship."
- Glaser, *Coming Out to God.*
- Storey, *Book of Prayer.*
- Stuart, "Making No Sense."

Pastoral Care
- Empereur, *Spiritual Direction and the Gay Person.*
- Graham, *Discovering Images of God.*
- Kundtz and Schlager, *Ministry Among God's Queer Folk.*
- Marshall, *Counseling Lesbian Partners.*
- Switzer, *Pastoral Care of Gays, Lesbians, and Their Families.*

Saints: Breaking Through of Radical Love

What is the significance of saints for LGBT people today? Are saints simply a quaint vestige of superstitious practices and popular religion? The Apostles' Creed refers to a belief in the "communion of saints," but what does that really mean? In fact, many LGBT people venerate special people as queer saints. These include traditional Christian saints such as the same-sex martyr couples of Saints Sergius and Bacchus and Saints Felicitas and Perpetua. Other traditional saints include Saint Aelred of Rievaulx, the monastic who wrote about the holiness of same-sex friendships.[37]

This practice of veneration may also include contemporary examples of queer martyrs and s/heroes such as the assassinated gay politician Harvey Milk, the late African American lesbian activist and poet Audre Lorde, and Father Mychal Judge, who ministered to the LGBT community and died in the 9/11 attacks on the World Trade Center. Other queer saints include those who have struggled to live and die in dignity with HIV/AIDS, and all the nameless queer people who have been killed because of hatred of trans and gender-variant people. Indeed, I have a number of reproductions of icons of queer saints painted by the remarkable artist Robert Lentz, OFM, on the door of my office.

From the perspective of queer theology, saints can be understood as the *breaking through of radical love*. That is, the doctrine of saints is highly queer because the saints dissolve all kinds of seemingly fixed boundaries: past vs. present, fantasy vs. reality, myth vs. history, the miraculous vs. the ordinary, and divine vs. human. Because of their radical love for God and neighbor, the saints are able to cross the boundaries of time and space in order to break into the lives of queer people today. Indeed, by venerating the saints, we affirm the radical love of God that dissolves all boundaries, including (but not limited to) sexuality and gender. Like the Holy Spirit, the lives of saints are a road map for us to return to God's radical love.

---

[37] See Martín Hugo Córdova Quero, "Friendship with Benefits: A Queer Reading of Aelred of Rievaulx and His Theology of Friendship," in *The Sexual Theologian: Essays on Sex, God and Politics*, ed. Marcella Althaus-Reid and Lisa Isherwood (London: T&T Clark International, 2004), 26–46.

Breaking through Erotic Boundaries

One way in which the saints break through radical love is by *breaking through erotic boundaries*. Donald Boisvert, a gay religious studies professor at Concordia University, has written a provocative book, *Sanctity and Male Desire: A Gay Reading of Saints*, about his homoerotic experience of the saints as an openly gay man with a Roman Catholic background. Although it might at first be surprising to connect the saints with same-sex erotic longing, there are in fact strong connections between sainthood and queer desire. Although Boisvert's own same-sex desire was expressly forbidden by the Roman Catholic Church, Boisvert's practice of venerating saints opened up a space for him in which such desire was encouraged and led to an "erotic fixation" on the saints from an early age.[38]

Based upon these experiences, Boisvert sets forth a number of queer readings of saints ranging from Michael the Archangel (as a "manly angel") to the martyrs Sebastian and Tarcisius (as archetypes of the "queer man divinized") to Father Damien of Molokai and the missionary saints (as symbols of conversion and seduction).[39] In his readings, Boisvert deliciously crosses the boundaries between fantasy and reality, past and present, and the holy and the erotic.

Boisvert concludes with a reflection of three categories of saints in the Roman Catholic Church—martyr, confessor, and doctor—and applies them to individuals in the LGBT community. For example, Boisvert sees the late Matthew Shepard, who was beaten to death and left to die on a fence in rural Wyoming, as an example of a contemporary queer martyr. By contrast, he sees the drag queens and other gender-variant people who initiated the Stonewall Riots and ushered in the modern-day queer-rights movement as examples of contemporary queer confessors (that is, saints marked by courage).

Finally, Boisvert sees queer thinkers such as the late philosopher Michel Foucault and late historian John Boswell as examples of contemporary queer doctors (to which I would

---

[38] Boisvert, *Sanctity and Male Desire*, 8.
[39] Boisvert, *Sanctity and Male Desire*, 38, 52, 152.

also add the late queer theorist Eve Kosofsky Sedgwick and the late queer theologian Marcella Althaus-Reid). For Boisvert, these saints operate by "flaunt[ing] established conventions" and serving as "virtuous, consecrated models" of queerness.[40] As such, these need not be established saints like Sergius and Bacchus or Aelred, but can be anyone who has been a role model for other LGBT people, or, in the words of the late Marcella Althaus-Reid, "sexual dissidents."[41]

Breaking through Literary Boundaries

A second way in which saints break through radical love is by *breaking through literary boundaries*. For example, Virginia Burrus has reflected on the relationship between the erotic and the saints in the context of hagiography (that is, the biographies of the saints). Burrus weaves together queer theory and imaginative readings of early Christian lives of the saints. As a result, Burrus collapses literary genres such as histories and queer romances.

For example, in "The Queer Life of Paul the Hermit," Burrus rereads Jerome's narrative of the meeting between Antony, the desert father, and Paul the Hermit as a queer romance. Akin to a same-sex courtship, Antony searches Paul out and begs repeatedly to be admitted to Paul's cave—even threatening to die in front of Paul's door before leaving. Eventually Antony breaks bread with Paul, which is described in erotic terms: "neither will be first, neither will top."[42] When Paul dies, Antony's grief is described in terms akin to the language of a lover. In fact, when Antony buries Paul, Antony takes on the position of a wife by wrapping Paul's body and carrying Paul's corpse to the grave.

In addition to challenging the boundaries between literary genres with respect to hagiography, Burrus also challenges the dualistic view that celibacy and sexuality are opposed to each other. For Burrus, eroticism is not erased in the case of the saints who remained celibate. Rather, it is *intensified* as

---

[40] Boisvert, *Sanctity and Male Desire*, 194–96.
[41] See Althaus-Reid, *Queer God*, 139–44 ("Queer Sainthood: Paths to Beatification for Sexual Dissidents").
[42] Burrus, *Sex Lives of Saints*, 31.

a result of the restraint shown by such individuals. In other words the "agonizing pleasure" of eroticism leads to a transcendence that dissolves the boundaries of the internal and the external. For Burrus, this is a form of *jouissance*, or erotic bliss.[43] Similarly, Lisa Isherwood has written about the "power of erotic celibacy," particularly with respect to the bodies of early Christian women, which were "prophetic sites of resistance to patriarchy."[44]

Mark Jordan has also written about the "sublimation of homoerotic desire" in the liturgical retellings of the story of the beautiful adolescent martyr Pelagius. According to tradition, Pelagius was tortured and executed because he resisted the sexual advances of an Islamic king so that he could remain chaste and a spouse to Jesus Christ. Jordan notes how Pelagius is transformed in Christian liturgical texts and art over time from a "naked ephebe into a triumphant military saint" because it would be too "obvious for celibate men to revere Pelagius as a naked 'athlete' or spouse of Christ."[45] Although the liturgical retellings attempt to suppress the homoerotic elements of the narrative, the allusions to same-sex desire are still embedded deeply in the literary genre of hagiography.

Breaking through Social Boundaries

A third way in which saints break through radical love is by *breaking through social boundaries*. Elizabeth Stuart has proposed a feminist theology of saints in *Spitting at Dragons: Towards a Feminist Theology of Sainthood*. Stuart admires the way in which many saints have broken through traditional barriers, including dualistic thinking and family boundaries. Stuart notes that the Christian cult of saints was "scandalous" in the ancient world because it challenged the boundaries between "earth and heaven, divinity and humanity, the living and the dead." Although non-Christians in the Roman Empire venerated the dead, they did not cross any "precious metaphysical boundaries" in terms of claiming any intimacy with the

[43] Burrus, *Sex Lives of Saints*, 14–15.
[44] Lisa Isherwood, *The Power of Erotic Celibacy: Queering Heteropatriarchy* (London: T&T Clark, 2006), 52.
[45] Jordan, *Invention of Sodomy*, 26.

divine.[46] Indeed, this boundary-crossing is at the heart of what queerness and radical love is all about!

Stuart also notes that the Christian cult of the saints challenged the traditional Roman role of the family and "boundary of kinship groups." Roman families took care of their own ancestors. However, the cult of saints allowed for such family lines to be crossed. In Stuart's words, "the dead belonged to everyone." Martyrs did not just belong to their biological families, but rather to the larger Christian community. Indeed, this practice deeply challenged social and family relationships that were grounded in patriarchy and "transcended all social boundaries."[47] As such, the practice of venerating saints—as well as Christianity itself—actually resulted in the dissolving of the boundary between family and strangers. The early Christians radically redefined the boundaries of family, which again is what lies at the heart of queerness and radical love.

This notion of sainthood as breaking through social boundaries is not limited to early Christians. In fact, contemporary saints include queer activists such as Sister Jeannine Gramick, a Roman Catholic nun with the Sisters of Loretto, who has devoted her life's work to ministering to the LGBT community. Despite being silenced by the Vatican, Sister Jeannine has continued to work fearlessly in a ministry of education and advocacy for LGBT people along with organizations such as New Ways Ministries, which she founded in 1977 with Father Robert Nugent.[48]

In sum, a theology of sainthood recognizes the radical love of those who have gone before us—and those who are still with us—who have broken through erotic, literary, and social boundaries. Indeed, these saints are witnesses to a love so radical that it is able to touch us through the normally impenetrable boundaries of time and space.

[46] Elizabeth Stuart, *Spitting at Dragons: Towards a Feminist Theology of Sainthood* (New York: Mowbray, 1996), 67.
[47] Stuart, *Spitting at Dragons*, 67.
[48] The website for New Ways Ministries is at http://www.newwaysministries.org. Sister Jeannine's work has been the subject of the documentary film *In Good Conscience: Sister Jeannine Gramick's Journey of Faith*. Some of Gramick's and Nugent's writings include Jeannine Gramick and Pat Furley, *The Vatican and Homosexuality: Reactions to the "Letter to the Bishops of the Catholic Church on the Pastoral Care of Homosexual Persons"* (New York: Crossroad, 1988); Jeannine Gramick and Robert Nugent, eds., *Voices of Hope: A Collection of Positive Catholic Writing on Gay and Lesbian Issues* (New York: Center for Homophobia Education, 1995); Robert Nugent, ed., *A Challenge to Love: Gay and Lesbian Catholics in the Church* (New York: Crossroad, 1984); and Robert Nugent and Jeannine Gramick, *Building Bridges: Gay and Lesbian Reality and the Catholic Church* (Mystic, CT: Twenty-Third Publications, 1992).

Study Questions

1. How can the doctrine of saints be understood as a celebration of the breaking through of radical love?

2. What are some ways in which queer saints have broken through erotic boundaries?

3. How have queer saints broken through literary boundaries?

4. How have queer saints broken through social boundaries? Who are some historical and contemporary saints for you?

For Further Study

Saints
- Althaus-Reid, "Queer Sainthood: Paths to Beatification for Sexual Dissidents."
- Boisvert, *Sanctity and Male Desire*.
- Burrus, *Sex Lives of Saints*.
- Halperin, *Saint Foucault*.
- Isherwood, *Power of Erotic Celibacy*.
- Stuart, *Spitting at Dragons*.

Sacraments: Foretaste of Radical Love

What do the sacraments mean for LGBT people? The classical definition of a sacrament is a visible sign of God's invisible grace. Assuming that God's grace is radical love (that is, a love so extreme that it dissolves existing boundaries), then the sacraments can be understood as a *foretaste of radical love*. Just as foreplay can be a foretaste of sexual pleasure, the sacraments can be a foretaste of our ultimate destiny when we are reunited with God's radical love. Indeed, at the end of the time, we will no longer have bodies that are marked by sex and gender. We will take on new spiritual bodies,[49] and the only identity that will matter is that we are members of the body of Christ. It is a function of the radical love of the Holy Spirit that brings us closer toward our eschatological destiny through the sacraments.

Is there an overarching sacrament for queer people? Chris Glaser argues that *coming out* is the central sacrament for LGBT people. According to Glaser, a sacrament—like the process of coming out—is a "*sensual* spiritual affair" that reminds us that "spirituality is not an out-of-body experience."[50] Indeed, the sacraments generally involve tangible matter such as water, bread, oil, and the like. Similarly, coming out frees us to be in true communion—through these senses of sight, sound, touch, taste, and smell—with other queer people. Furthermore, for Glaser, it is only through the coming out process that God's invisible grace is made visible.

For Protestants, there are two sacraments: baptism and Eucharist. For Roman Catholics, however, there are an additional five sacraments: confirmation, reconciliation, matrimony, holy orders, and anointing of the sick. (Protestants recognize only the two sacraments of baptism and Eucharist because they believe that those are the only ones that are grounded explicitly in scripture.) This section will cover each of the seven sacraments from the perspective of queer theology.

---

[49] 1 Cor. 15:44.
[50] Glaser, *Coming Out as Sacrament*, 5 (emphasis in original).

Baptism

Baptism is the initiation or welcoming rite into the Christian church, and it is conferred by pouring water over the head of the individual or immersing the individual in water. Traditionally understood, baptism is a sign of dying to one's old life and being born again into a new life. According to Glaser, coming out is like baptism in that LGBT people let their old closeted lives die and are born into a new life.[51]

For Elizabeth Stuart, the sacrament of baptism is fundamentally queer because, theologically speaking, it wipes out all distinctions of gender, sexuality, and other markers of identity. That is, the only thing that matters upon being baptized is one's membership in the body of Christ. Stuart notes that baptism unmasks the "inadequacy of all other forms of identity" and is grounded in a "radical equality" that arises out of the fact that our existence is due to God's grace alone.[52] Indeed, baptism can be a useful locus of reflection for queer people. Not only can the sacrament be conferred by lay people, but the priesthood of all the baptized washes away all distinctions within the body of Christ.[53] In that context, none of the various identities that lead to church-sanctioned exclusion (for example, gender or sexuality) matter.[54]

Mark Jordan underscores this point in an essay called "'Baptizing' Queer Characters." He argues that our various identities—including those relating to sexual orientation—do not matter in the end. For Jordan, it is important that LGBT people are not "trapped, reduced, or divided" by them. That is, "no one of us *is* an invert, a homophile, a homosexual—not simply, not finally."[55] And that is the fundamental truth of which baptism reminds us.

---

[51] Glaser, *Coming Out as Sacrament*, 12.

[52] Stuart, "Sacramental Flesh," 67.

[53] For a discussion of the ministry of the baptized, see Sheryl A. Kujawa-Holbrook and Fredrica Harris Thompsett, *Born of Water, Born of Spirit: Supporting the Ministry of the Baptized in Small Congregations* (Herndon, VA: Alban Institute, 2010). See also M. Thomas Shaw, *Conversations with Scripture and with Each Other: Spiritual Formation for Lay Leaders* (Lanham, MD: Rowman and Littlefield, 2008).

[54] This is reinforced by the ancient baptismal formula in Gal. 3:28 that "[t]here is no longer Jew or Greek, there is no longer slave or free, there is no longer male and female; for all of you are one in Christ Jesus." See also Elizabeth Stuart, "Sexuality: The View from the Font," *Theology and Sexuality*, no. 11 (Sept. 1999): 16 ("Baptism incorporates a person into a new community and cultural context that relativizes and radicalizes their relationship to all other social institutions and that includes the family").

[55] Mark D. Jordan, "'Baptizing' Queer Characters," in Kamitsuka, *Embrace of Eros*, 163.

Eucharist

The second sacrament is the Eucharist or the Lord's Supper. Although the various Christian denominations differ on what the Eucharist is (that is, whether the bread and wine are actually transubstantiated into the body and blood of Jesus Christ, whether it is simply a memorial of the Last Supper, or whether it is something in between), the denominations do agree that participating in the sacrament of Eucharist signifies belonging to the larger body of Christ.

A number of LGBT theologians have focused upon the communal nature of the Eucharist. For Chris Glaser, the act of coming out is most like the sacrament of Eucharist because "both involve a sacrifice and offering that creates at-one-ment or communion with God and with others."[56] For Robert Shore-Goss, both sex and the Eucharist are "intimate and sacred moments of lovemaking." That is, Shore-Goss has written about the "intimacy" of the "communion" between him and his partner as that which actually "infused both the bedroom and the altar."[57]

For Elizabeth Stuart, however, the Eucharist is fundamentally queer because it symbolizes the erasure of sex in a number of ways. For example, the traditional eastward-facing or *ad orientem* position of the Roman Catholic priest (who is wearing the traditional chasuble, which is also a nongendered garment) has the effect of erasing the sex of the priest because both the priest and the congregation are facing in the same direction. Furthermore, the priest who acts *in persona Christi*, or in the person of Christ, is actually transforming the body of Christ into something sexless by the act of consecrating bread and wine. Furthermore, to the extent that the body of Christ *is* the church, this body is made up of a multitude of sexes, genders, and other identities that are rendered nonultimate in the new creation. As such, the Eucharist for Stuart reveals that "for the baptized, sex, gender, sexuality and all other forms of identity by which humans categorize themselves are not of ultimate concern."[58]

---

[56] Glaser, *Coming Out as Sacrament*, 15.
[57] Goss, "Passionate Love for Christ," 302.
[58] Stuart, "Priest at the Altar," 136.

For Stuart, the Eucharist is like baptism in that it anticipates the "eschatological life" in which "gender and the sexual identities built upon it are rendered non-ultimate."[59] She cites the theology of Gregory of Nyssa for the proposition that humans will return to a sexless angel-like state (that is, what humans were like before the fall) in the general resurrection. As such, sexualities and gender identities ultimately do not matter. As such, the sacrament of the Eucharist serves to dissolve the boundaries between female and male, which makes it a manifestation of radical love.

Confirmation

Each of the other five sacraments that are recognized by the Roman Catholic Church can also be viewed in queer terms. For example, the sacrament of confirmation—which marks our entry into adulthood and confirms our place in the church—is about radical love because it dissolves the boundaries between insider and outsider. Confirmation is connected with coming out because both acts allow us to affirm our place in God's realm. In coming out, we choose to become part of the larger LGBT community. Similarly, confirmation allows us to "begin to confirm our faith that we too are citizens of God's spiritual commonwealth."[60]

Robert Shore-Goss also understands the significance of confirmation in terms of formalizing one's membership in the LGBT community. Like baptism, this sacrament of initiation allows queer Christians to "move into shared erotic power for justice with other gay/lesbian Christians."[61] Elizabeth Stuart tells a rather queer story about her own confirmation at the age of eleven; when she was asked to choose a new name for her confirmation (as Roman Catholic children do), she chose "Augustine," a gender-transgressing name that represented for her a saint who was "assertive, active, influential, and a theologian."[62] All of these queer theological reflections on the sacrament of confirmation affirm our place as LGBT people in the realm of God.

[59] Stuart, "Sacramental Flesh," 71.
[60] Glaser, *Coming Out as Sacrament*, 14.
[61] Goss, *Jesus Acted Up*, 129, 131.
[62] Stuart, *Spitting at Dragons*, ix.

Reconciliation

The fourth sacrament is reconciliation. This sacrament—which is also known as penance—involves the absolution, or forgiveness, of one's sins. The process usually involves some kind of confession of sin as well as some act of penance. The sacrament of reconciliation is about radical love because it dissolves the boundaries between guilt and innocence. The sacrament of reconciliation is also closely connected with coming out. In coming out, we "repent of the closet" as well as its "myriad sinful expressions" such as dishonest behavior or exploiting others. Our penance is a positive thing: it is "accepting God's gift of our sexuality" and being honest with others about who we are.[63]

Robert Shore-Goss also draws the connection between reconciliation and the queer experience. Specifically, reconciliation means not just repentance on the part of LGBT people, but also the refusal of queer Christians to be reconciled with churches that still engage in "heterosexist oppression" and "compulsory heterosexuality."[64] This is particularly the case with the Roman Catholic Church, which has chosen to deflect attention away from its failure to maintain a "healthy sexual ethic" and instead scapegoat queer people for the clergy sexual abuse scandal of recent years.[65]

Matrimony

The fifth sacrament is matrimony, or marriage, and has been the subject of much writing by queer theologians in recent years. Matrimony is the sacred covenanting of two persons who promise their fidelity in love to each other before God and their community. Matrimony is about radical love because it dissolves the boundaries between the self and other. The sacrament of matrimony is also closely connected with coming out because coming out is precisely what makes same-sex marriages possible in the first place.[66] In other words, only when we open

---

[63] Glaser, *Coming Out as Sacrament*, 13.
[64] Goss, *Jesus Acted Up*, 135.
[65] See Donald L. Boisvert and Robert E. Goss, eds., *Gay Catholic Priests and Clerical Sexual Misconduct: Breaking the Silence* (Binghamton, NY: Harrington Park Press, 2005), 1; see also Jordan, *Telling Truths in Church*.
[66] Glaser, *Coming Out as Sacrament*, 15.

ourselves up by sharing our sexualities and gender identities with others are we then able to develop the kind of authentic relationships that can lead to a covenantal marriage.

For Robert Shore-Goss, same-sex unions, including same-sex marriages, are sacred because they often exist without the same "heterosexist power relations or conjugal stereotypes" that occur within heterosexual marriage. For example, Michael and I have a division of household chores (he cooks, I do the dishes) and caring for our dog (he walks her at night, I walk her in the morning) that is based upon what works for us and not gender roles or preconceived notions. Furthermore, Shore-Goss argues that same-sex unions are sacramental because they recognize the couple's union as "sexual praxis, sexual action committed to God's reign."[67]

In recent years there have been a number of works on the theology, history, and ethics of same-sex marriage, including *As My Own Soul: The Blessing of Same-Gender Marriage*; *Authorizing Marriage?: Canon, Tradition, and Critique in the Blessing of Same-Sex Unions*; *Blessing Same-Sex Unions: The Perils of Queer Romance and the Confusions of Christian Marriage*; *The Friend*; *Reasonable and Holy: Engaging Same-Sexuality*; *Same-Sex Marriage?: A Christian Ethical Analysis*; *Same-Sex Unions in Premodern Europe*; and *What God Has Joined Together?: A Christian Case for Gay Marriage*.[68] These works are particularly timely in light of the various civil jurisdictions around the world that have recognized same-sex marriages in whole or in part, including Argentina, Belgium, Canada, Iceland, Mexico, Netherlands, Norway, Portugal, South Africa, Spain, Sweden, and the United States.

There have also been many queer theological writings on same-sex marriage, including the description by Gerard Loughlin of the surprising medieval tradition of depicting Jesus

---

[67] Goss, *Jesus Acted Up*, 138.
[68] See Chris Glaser, *As My Own Soul: The Blessing of Same-Gender Marriage* (New York: Seabury Books, 2009); Jordan, *Authorizing Marriage?*; Mark D. Jordan, *Blessing Same-Sex Unions: The Perils of Queer Romance and the Confusions of Christian Marriage* (Chicago: University of Chicago Press, 2005); Bray, *The Friend*; Tobias Stanislas Haller, *Reasonable and Holy: Engaging Same-Sexuality* (New York: Seabury Books, 2009); Marvin M. Ellison, *Same-Sex Marriage?: A Christian Ethical Analysis* (Cleveland, OH: Pilgrim Press, 2004); Boswell, *Same-Sex Unions in Premodern Europe*; and David G. Myers and Letha Dawson Scanzoni, *What God Has Joined Together?: A Christian Case for Gay Marriage* (San Francisco: HarperSanFrancisco, 2005).

and John the Beloved Disciple as the unnamed couple who were married at Cana,[69] as well as a provocative roundtable discussion in the *Journal of Feminist Studies in Religion* among Mary E. Hunt, Marvin M. Ellison, Emilie M. Townes, Martha Ackelsberg, Judith Plaskow, Angela Bauer-Levesque, and me over whether same-sex marriage simply reinforces patriarchy or is indeed a new creation.[70]

Scott Haldeman, a gay professor at Chicago Theological Seminary, has proposed "queer fidelity" as a new ethical norm for Christian marriage and challenges monogamy as the sole norm for marriages.[71] Finally, Elizabeth Stuart has described marriage as an institution that parallels the union between Jesus Christ and the church, which in turns brings the church into the Trinity. Because there is no "procreative principle" within the Trinity, Stuart argues that the heart of the sacrament of marriage should be covenant and not procreation. In any event, human marriage (whether same-sex or opposite-sex) is not of ultimate significance because it ends at death and ceases to exist at the consummation of all things.[72]

Holy Orders

The sixth sacrament is holy orders, which is the ordination of a person to serve God in the preaching of the word and celebrating of the sacraments. Holy orders is about radical love because it dissolves the boundaries between the divine and human, particularly given the mediating function of the priest or minister. Like the sacrament of matrimony, the sacrament of holy orders has created much division in the mainline Protestant churches, particularly following the episcopal consecration in 2003 of V. Eugene Robinson, the first openly gay and openly partnered individual to be elected and consecrated a bishop in the Episcopal Church and the wider Anglican Communion.[73] (Bishop Robinson was followed in

---

[69] Loughlin, "Introduction," 1–4.

[70] See "Roundtable Discussion: Same-Sex Marriage," *Journal of Feminist Studies in Religion* 20, no. 2 (Fall 2004): 83–117.

[71] See Scott Haldeman, "A Queer Fidelity: Reinventing Christian Marriage," *Theology and Sexuality* 13, no. 2 (Jan. 2007): 137–52; see also Susan Dowell, "Challenging Monogamy," *Theology and Sexuality*, no. 2 (March 1995): 84–103.

[72] Stuart, "Sacramental Flesh," 72–73.

[73] See Elizabeth Adams, *Going to Heaven: The Life and Election of Bishop Gene Robinson* (Brooklyn, NY: Soft Skull Press, 2006); see also Andrew Linzey and Richard Kirker, *Gays and the Future of Anglicanism: Responses to the Windsor Report* (Winchester, UK: O Books, 2005).

2010 with the election and consecration of the Right Reverend Mary Glasspool, the first out and partnered lesbian bishop in the Episcopal Church.) Similar controversy has followed the decision of the Evangelical Lutheran Church in America in the summer of 2010 to allow the ordination of ministers who live in same-sex relationships.

For Chris Glaser, the sacrament of holy orders is closely connected with coming out because both involve a ministry of presence that bears witness to "God's inclusive love, God's creative diversity, spiritual-sexual integrity, and harmony among sexual orientation." Indeed, Glaser notes that there are many "sacred callings" for LGBT people.[74] For example, the gay Episcopal priest and theologian L. William Countryman has written about the many gifts that LGBT people bring to the church, including what he calls "our particular priesthood" of being a blessing to ourselves and others, being an odd sort of minority, being sexual, being friends, being family, and being alive in the face of death.[75]

Other queer theologians have written about different aspects of holy orders. For Robert Shore-Goss, the sacrament of ordination is a *rejection* of power and domination over others. Rather, queer ministers are called to "love-making" and "justice-doing" and an exercise of authority that is "symmetrical and egalitarian."[76] Eleanor McLaughlin, the Episcopal priest, has written about the woman priest as a cross-dresser—that is, a "woman dressed as a man dressed as a woman"—and also as an icon of the Jesus Christ with "transvestic sensibilities."[77] Elizabeth Stuart has written provocatively about how the Roman Catholic priest is a "transsexual," or one who, by facing the liturgical east along with the people, "embodies, anticipates and leads into a divine life beyond sex."[78]

[74] Glaser, *Coming Out as Sacrament*, 14–15.
[75] See William L. Countryman and M.R. Ritley, *Gifted by Otherness: Gay and Lesbian Christians in the Church* (Harrisburg, PA: Morehouse Publishing, 2001), 139–49.
[76] Goss, *Jesus Acted Up*, 139.
[77] McLaughlin, "Feminist Christologies," 142–43.
[78] Stuart, "Priest at the Altar," 134–35.

Anointing of the Sick

The seventh and final sacrament is the anointing of the sick. This sacrament—previously called last rites—is a sacrament of healing. It is about radical love because it dissolves the boundaries between sickness and health. For Chris Glaser, the anointing of the sick is closely connected with coming out in that both are about healing, whether it is the healing of our bodies, our internalized homophobia, or our broken relationships.[79] Similarly, Shore-Goss draws a connection between the anointing of the sick and rites of healing in the queer community's outreach to HIV-positive people (as opposed to the silence and lack of action by many churches, which Shore-Goss characterizes as "morally bankrupt"). Shore-Goss quotes a leather jacket of an HIV-positive person that says "God is HIV +." For Shore-Goss, this notion of an HIV-positive God asserts "God's solidarity with HIV-infected people, their marginalization, and suffering."[80] Robert Williams also has written about the connections between HIV/AIDS, the sacraments, and healing. For Williams, liturgical sacraments such as the anointing of the sick are a "distillation of what was once much more elaborate," but are still helpful to the extent that they channel the healing energy of the Holy Spirit.[81]

Summary

In conclusion, Mark Jordan aptly describes the Christian sacraments as being fundamentally queer. He notes that Christianity, as expressed through its sacramental actions, is a religion of "exchanging identities without sex" and can achieve this only through "multiple substitutions of identity." According to Jordan, "at the Mass, a priest becomes Christ, but also Christ's spouse; a nun at her veiling becomes the virgin martyr Agnes, but also Christ's bride. In baptism, the new believer puts on Christ; in the Eucharist, she or he consumes Christ as bread and wine in order to be united with Christ."[82] These substitutions point to the ultimate instability of identities. These are examples

---

[79] See Glaser, *Coming Out as Sacrament*, 14.
[80] Goss, *Jesus Acted Up*, 135.
[81] Williams, *Just as I Am*, 266–67.
[82] Jordan, "Sodomites and Churchmen," 240.

of how the sacraments dissolve the boundaries between female and male, divine and human, guilt and innocence, punishment and reward, and other binary categories, and therefore provide us with a foretaste of the radical love to come.

Study Questions

1. How are sacraments a foretaste of radical love? What is your experience with sacramental religious traditions such as Roman Catholicism or Anglicanism?

2. What are some connections between coming out and the traditional Christian sacraments (baptism, Eucharist, confirmation, reconciliation, matrimony, holy orders, and the anointing of the sick)?

3. How is baptism a marker of radical equality? How well does the church live up to this standard in practice?

4. How does the Eucharist anticipate the world to come in which our sexual and gender identities are no longer of ultimate significance?

5. What are some ways in which LGBT people confirm their membership in the LGBT community?

6. What would it take for homophobic or heterosexist religious traditions to be reconciled to the LGBT community?

7. What is your view about the theological significance of same-sex marriage? Do you believe that same-sex marriage ultimately liberates LGBT people or, on the other hand, is restrictive and devalues other kinds of queer relationships?

8. How do LGBT individuals who receive holy orders bear witness to God's inclusive love?

9. How is the anointing of the sick an act of radical love for LGBT people, including those with HIV/AIDS?

For Further Study

Sacraments

Generally
- Glaser, *Coming Out as Sacrament*, 7–15.
- Goss, *Jesus Acted Up*, 126–41.
- Stuart, "Sacramental Flesh."
- Williams, *Just as I Am*, 127–39.

Baptism
- Jordan, "'Baptizing' Queer Characters."
- Stuart, "Sacramental Flesh," 66–68.
- Williams, *Just as I Am*, 131–33.

Eucharist
- Goss, "Passionate Love for Christ."
- Stuart, "Priest at the Altar."
- Williams, *Just as I Am*, 133–35.

Confirmation
- Glaser, *Coming Out as Sacrament*, 13–14.
- Goss, *Jesus Acted Up*, 128–32.

Reconciliation
- Glaser, *Coming Out as Sacrament*, 13.
- Goss, *Jesus Acted Up*, 134–36.
- Williams, *Just as I Am*, 166–68 ("Confession"; "Reconciliation").

Matrimony
- Ellison, *Same-Sex Marriage?*
- Glaser, *As My Own Soul*.
- Haller, *Reasonable and Holy*.
- Jordan, *Authorizing Marriage?*.
- Jordan, *Blessing Same-Sex Unions*.
- Williams, *Just as I Am*, 135–39.

Holy Orders
- Countryman and Ritley, *Gifted by Otherness*, 139–49.
- McLaughlin, "Feminist Christologies."
- Stuart, "Priest at the Altar."

Anointing of the Sick
- Glaser, *Coming Out as Sacrament*, 14.
- Goss, *Jesus Acted Up*, 134–36.
- Williams, *Just as I Am*, 263–67 ("Christian Healing"; "Sharing Energy").

Last Things: Horizon of Radical Love

The last topic in this book is that of Christian last things, or eschatology. For many queer people, the doctrine of eschatology—which includes matters such as the second coming of Jesus Christ, the Last Judgment, heaven, and hell—raises a number of difficult issues, particularly since many of us have been told from a young age that we are going to hell because of our sexualities and/or gender identities. As such, it is not surprising that LGBT theologians often do not address this doctrine in their theologies.

Ironically, however, the doctrine of last things may be the queerest doctrine of all because it is the ultimate return to the radical love from which we originally came. That is, if radical love is defined as a love that is so extreme that it dissolves all boundaries, then the ultimate dissolution of identities is what will occur at the end of time. As such, the doctrine of last things can be understood as the *horizon of radical love* to which we are all directed or oriented.

Eschatological Erasure of Female and Male

Elizabeth Stuart demonstrates how eschatology is central to the enterprise of queer theology. At the end of time, when we take on "spiritual bodies,"[83] our human identities will no longer matter—including those of sexuality and gender. In other words, all of our fixed identities will be obliterated. The only thing that matters in the end is our membership in the body of Christ. Interestingly, Stuart argues that only the Christian theologian can respond to the queer theorist Judith Butler and affirm that there actually *is* a place where one can be truly queer, and thus avoid a fate of "self-destructive despair." That place is the "eschatological horizon" of the church that affirms that "gender and sexual identity are not of ultimate concern, thus opening the possibility for love."[84]

Stuart relies upon the work of Sarah Coakley, who cites the fourth-century Cappadocian theologian Gregory of Nyssa

---

[83] 1 Cor. 15:44.
[84] Stuart, "Sacramental Flesh," 65.

to demonstrate the connection between queer theory and the gender fluidity of this eschatological horizon.[85] For Stuart, "in the end" there is "only one identity stable enough to hope in." That identity is being a baptized member of the body of Christ, an identity that puts all other "secular identities" under "eschatological erasure." According to Stuart, the body of Christ "parodies and subverts all culturally constructed identities," which ultimately leaves us with the realization that "in Christ maleness and femaleness and gay and straight are categories that dissolve before the throne of grace where only the garment of baptism remains."[86] In other words, we are all transgender in the end.[87]

It should be noted, however, that this does *not* require that we be completely absorbed into God at the eschaton and that our individual selves cease to exist. As we have seen above, Susannah Cornwall, drawing upon the work of Sarah Coakley and Gregory of Nyssa, suggests that the human journey toward God is a process of "continual journeying." As such, while we may approach God's perfection, we will never arrive—even at the eschaton—at any "climactic picture of perfection."[88] Thus, the fundamental distinction between God and humanity is preserved while at the same time the relationship between God and humanity is always drawing closer.

Eschatological Erasure of Life and Death

One of the most significant events for LGBT theologians with respect to the doctrine of last things has been the devastating effect of HIV/AIDS on the gay male community. During the early 1980s through the mid-1990s (when the discovery of protease inhibitors dramatically increased the lifespan of people with HIV/AIDS), gay men were faced with the issue of death and afterlife on a constant basis. However, despite the empirical evidence that an overwhelming number of gay men with HIV/AIDS had well thought out views of life after

---

[85] See Sarah Coakley, "The Eschatological Body: Gender, Transformation, and God," *Modern Theology* 16, no. 1 (Jan. 2000), 70–71.

[86] Stuart, "Sacramental Flesh," 74–75.

[87] But see Mark D. Jordan, "God's Body," in Loughlin, *Queer Theology*, 290 (arguing that the post-resurrection body will be "the best human bodies there are, which means, as bodies with genitals").

[88] Cornwall, "Apophasis and Ambiguity," 25–28.

death—including a strong belief in life after death—many gay and lesbian theologians were silent about issues of eschatology or last things in their theologies. According to Elizabeth Stuart, this was due to the fact that these theologians were "paralysed by pre-existing theological paradigms and assumptions which they could only repeat."[89]

A number of gay male theologians did address the issue of last things explicitly, however. For example, Robert Williams, who ultimately died of complications from HIV/AIDS himself, argued that whether or not the afterlife exists "makes a hell of a lot of difference." According to Williams (writing in the early 1990s), this is true because "unless you are truly isolated from your community, you have been to a lot of funerals and memorial services lately."[90] Williams wrote that he would not be able to "deal with the reality of AIDS" without the "sure and certain hope of the resurrection."[91] For Williams, belief in the resurrection is not a matter of proof, but rather simply a matter of faith.

John Fortunato, an openly gay psychotherapist, also acknowledged that any book about HIV/AIDS and spirituality would have to discuss the question of immortality. In "A Case for Heaven," one of the chapters in his book *AIDS, the Spiritual Dilemma*, Fortunato navigates between the two extremes of the post-Enlightenment mindset (that is, rejecting all heaven talk) and the fundamentalist mindset (that is, having only a biblical view of heaven). Fortunato uses examples from contemporary physics to demonstrate that, at the most basic level, the actions of atoms and other particles are "shrouded in mystery" and uncertainty.[92] That is, when human knowledge is pushed to its limits, the empirical language of science fails. Perhaps, Fortunato suggests, our basic human intuition about the existence of heaven, afterlife, and the mysteries of the cosmos may in fact be the right answer.

John McNeill also addressed the effects of the HIV/AIDS pandemic upon the LGBT community. McNeill wrote about

---

[89] Stuart, *Gay and Lesbian Theologies*, 75.
[90] Williams, *Just as I Am*, 280.
[91] Williams, *Just as I Am*, 281.
[92] Fortunato, *AIDS, the Spiritual Dilemma*, 134.

how HIV/AIDS has forced all people to face the reality of human mortality. He notes that most heterosexual couples satisfy the basic human urge to transcend human finitude and mortality through reproduction. However, because this option is often not available to many LGBT people (at least without substantial technological and other resources), this gives them the choice to either (1) despair or (2) accept the hope of the resurrection of the dead. And it is the special "spiritual peace, joy, and trust" that McNeill saw in his patients with HIV/AIDS that has allowed such people to hope in the resurrection and to "give themselves over to celebrating life and enhancing its quality for themselves and others."[93]

A number of other gay theologians have also tried to reclaim the doctrine of last things through the lens of queer experience. Michael Vasey, a gay Anglican priest and liturgist at the University of Durham, wrote about the "new cultural dialogue with death" that arose out of the HIV/AIDS pandemic.[94] In a chapter of his book *Strangers and Friends: A New Exploration of Homosexuality and the Bible* entitled "Over the Rainbow," Vasey notes that there is no marriage in heaven,[95] so LGBT people (who could not get married in the mid-1990s, when Vasey's book was written) would not feel excluded. Furthermore, Vasey notes how traditional images of heaven are so grand that they are "almost camp" and also have a lot in common with a gay pride event![96]

Ronald E. Long, an openly gay theologian who teaches at Hunter College in New York City, has wrestled with the question of whether there is sex in heaven. Long argues that, to the extent that heaven represents the "satisfactions of the desire of the human heart," and to the extent that sex is "one of the deepest and most profound of human motivations," then there must be sex in heaven.[97] However, Long argues that this sex is paradoxically neither an orgy nor polyamorous in nature.

---

[93] McNeill, *Taking a Chance on God*, 156.
[94] Michael Vasey, *Strangers and Friends: A New Exploration of Homosexuality and the Bible* (London: Hodder and Stoughton, 1995), 238.
[95] See Matt. 22:30.
[96] Vasey, *Strangers and Friends*, 248.
[97] Ronald E. Long, "Heavenly Sex: The Moral Authority of an Impossible Dream," *Theology and Sexuality* 11, no. 3 (May 2005): 39.

Rather, it is the *couple* that is the sexual ideal because truly great sex inevitably leads to wanting more with the same person. For Long, good sex provides the "opening, the invitation, to the repeat performance which is the ground of relationship."[98] Robert Williams also discusses whether there is sex in heaven. Williams imagines that, because sex in heaven is not physical, "you actually can enter the whole person. It's like you are in fact merging—becoming one."[99]

The foregoing reflections by gay male theologians about eschatology—arising for the most part out of their attempts to make sense of the horrifying HIV/AIDS pandemic—are ultimately about radical love because our hope in the resurrection of the dead dissolves the very boundaries between life and death.

Eschatological Erasure of Punishment and Reward

Finally, queer theology must wrestle with the question of the Last Judgment, and issues of eternal punishment or reward, particularly since so many LGBT people are told that we will be condemned to eternal suffering for engaging in same-sex acts. I believe that if radical love is to triumph in the end, then *all* barriers that separate us from God will be dissolved, including those of punishment and reward. For me, the second-century theologian Origen had it right in terms of his doctrine of *apokatastasis*, or the restoration of all things. According to this doctrine, if God is truly sovereign, then good must decisively triumph over evil in the end, which would mean that even Satan is saved. This does not mean that people will not need to be purified before reaching heaven—just as gold needs to be refined by fire—but, in the end, all will reach heaven.

Not all queer theologians subscribe to this view of the Last Judgment. For example, John McNeill proposes another view. For McNeill, the Last Judgment is actually a question of self-judgment in terms of how we have related to God during our lifetimes. He describes C.S. Lewis's depiction of creatures either running away from or toward the lion Aslan, depending

[98] Long, "Heavenly Sex," 43.
[99] Williams, *Just as I Am*, 285.

upon whether they hated or loved him during their lifetimes. The creatures who run away from Aslan end up running into the darkness. However, the creatures who run toward Aslan run into the light.[100] Thus, the Last Judgment for McNeill is a matter of self-selection. For me, however, this view is not satisfactory because it does not recognize the ultimate dissolving of boundaries—including the line between punishment vs. reward, or guilt vs. innocence—and the ultimate triumph of God's radical love.

According to the doctrine of *apokatastasis*, all things will be restored because of the ultimate triumph of God over evil and death. As we have seen, the boundaries between female and male, life and death, and punishment and reward will be subject to eschatological erasure at the end of time. Indeed, even the boundaries between the different world religions will be erased. Through the trajectory of salvation history, we have traveled from God (the one who sends forth radical love) to Jesus Christ (the one who recovers the radical love that we have lost) and to the Holy Spirit (the one who returns us to radical love). As St. Paul promises us, nothing can ever separate us from the love of God.[101] It is hard to imagine any love that is more radical than that!

[100] McNeill, *Taking a Chance on God*, 165.
[101] Rom. 8:38–39.

Study Questions

1. How can the doctrine of last things be understood as pointing to the horizon of radical love?

2. In what way does Christian eschatology erase the boundaries between female and male? Life and death? Punishment and reward?

3. Is it the case that our separate identities as human beings must be merged into God at the eschaton?

4. What role did the HIV/AIDS pandemic in the 1980s and 1990s (and continuing to this day) play with respect to the reflection upon last things by queer theologians, including HIV-positive theologians?

5. What is your view of the doctrine of last things, including heaven, hell, and the Last Judgment? Does the doctrine of *apokatastasis*, or the restoration of all things, appeal to you? Why or why not?

For Further Study

Last Things
- Coakley, "Eschatological Body."
- Fortunato, *AIDS, the Spiritual Dilemma*, 119–41 ("A Case for Heaven").
- Long, "Heavenly Sex."
- McNeill, *Taking a Chance on God*, 145–75 ("Unto Dust You Shall Return").
- Stuart, *Gay and Lesbian Theologies*, 65–77 ("AIDS and the Failure of Gay and Lesbian Theology").
- Stuart, "Queering Death."
- Stuart, *Sacramental Flesh*.
- Vasey, *Strangers and Friends*, 238–50 ("Over the Rainbow").
- Williams, *Just as I Am*, 276–85 ("Sure and Certain Hope: Death and Afterlife").

Conclusion

As I stated at the beginning of this book, Christian theology is fundamentally a queer enterprise. That is, like queer theory, classical Christian theology is about the breaking down of traditionally fixed boundaries and categories. For example, the doctrines of revelation, creation, and incarnation break down the allegedly fixed boundaries that separate the divine from the human. The doctrines of the resurrection and last things break down the allegedly fixed boundaries that separate death from life. The doctrine of atonement breaks down the allegedly fixed boundaries that separate guilt and innocence. And so on.

As such, the organizing idea for this book has been "radical love," which is defined as a love that is so extreme that it dissolves all existing boundaries, including those boundaries relating to sexuality and gender. I have argued that Christian theology can be understood as a three-part drama about radical love:

- the first act involves God, who is the *sending forth of radical love*;

- the second act involves Jesus Christ, who is the *recovery of the radical love that was lost by humans*; and

- the third act involves the Holy Spirit, who is the means by which we *return to radical love.*

Radical love is what bridges the gap between queer theory and Christian theology. It is my hope that this book will encourage its readers to explore further the amazing world of queer theology and to do some queer theologizing of their own. If this book has resulted in dissolving some of the boundaries that historically have separated Christianity and queerness, spirituality and sexuality, and soul and body, then it will have succeeded in pointing the way to the eschatological erasure that is our ultimate destiny.

In sum, Christian theology is ultimately about radical love. It affirms the impossibly queer truth that God is love, that God's very self is an internal community of love, that God's love spilled forth in the act of creation, that God became human out of God's love for humanity, and that God continues to guide us back toward the love from whence we came. Christian theology promises us that *nothing*—not hardship, not distress, not persecution, not famine, not nakedness, not peril, not the sword, not death, not life, not angels, not rulers, not things present, not things to come, not powers, not height, not depth, nor anything else in creation—can *ever* separate us from the love of God.[1] There is no love that is more radical than that, and that is why Christian theology is, at its core, a queer enterprise.

---

[1] Rom. 8:35–39.

Bibliography

Adams, Elizabeth. *Going to Heaven: The Life and Election of Bishop Gene Robinson*. Brooklyn, NY: Soft Skull Press, 2006.

Alison, James. *Broken Hearts and New Creations: Intimations of a Great Reversal*. London: Continuum, 2010.

_____. *Faith Beyond Resentment: Fragments Catholic and Gay*. New York: Crossroad Publishing, 2001.

_____. "The Gay Thing: Following the Still Small Voice." In Loughlin, *Queer Theology*, 50–62.

_____. *The Joy of Being Wrong: Original Sin Through Easter Eyes*. New York: Crossroad Publishing, 1998.

_____. *On Being Liked*. New York: Crossroad Publishing, 2003.

_____. "The Place of Shame and the Giving of the Spirit." In Alison, *Undergoing God*, 199–219.

_____. *Undergoing God: Dispatches from the Scene of a Break-In*. New York: Continuum, 2006.

Alpert, Rebecca. *Like Bread on the Seder Plate: Jewish Lesbians and the Transformation of Tradition*. New York: Columbia University Press, 1997.

Althaus-Reid, Marcella. *From Feminist Theology to Indecent Theology*. London: SCM Press, 2004.

_____. *Indecent Theology: Theological Perversions in Sex, Gender and Politics*. London: Routledge, 2000.

_____, ed. *Liberation Theology and Sexuality*. Aldershot, UK: Ashgate, 2006.

_____. *The Queer God*. London: Routledge, 2003.

Althaus-Reid, Marcella, and Lisa Isherwood, eds. *Controversies in Body Theology*. London: SCM Press, 2008.

_____, eds. *Controversies in Feminist Theology*. London: SCM Press, 2007.

_____, eds. *The Sexual Theologian: Essays on Sex, God and Politics*. London: T&T Clark International, 2004.

_____, eds. *Trans/formations*. London: SCM Press, 2009.

Anderson, Lisa Ann. "Desiring to Be Together: A Theological Reflection on Friendship Between Black Lesbians and Gay Men." *Theology and Sexuality*, no. 9 (Sept. 1998): 59–63.

Anderson, Victor. "African American Church Traditions." In Siker, *Homosexuality and Religion*, 48–50.

Armour, Ellen T., and Susan M. St. Ville, eds. *Bodily Citations: Religion and Judith Butler*. New York: Columbia University Press, 2006.

Arpin, Robert L. *Wonderfully, Fearfully Made: Letters on Living with Hope, Teaching Understanding, and Ministering with Love, from a Gay Catholic Priest with AIDS*. San Francisco: HarperSanFrancisco, 1993.

Auger, Jeanette A. *Passing Through: The End-of-Life Decisions of Lesbians and Gay Men*. Halifax, Canada: Fernwood Publishing, 2003.

Bagemihl, Bruce. *Biological Exuberance: Animal Homosexuality and Natural Diversity*. New York: St. Martin's Press, 1999.

Bailey, Derrick Sherwin. *Homosexuality and the Western Christian Tradition*. London: Longmans, Green, 1955.

Bailey, Randall C., Tat-siong Benny Liew, and Fernando F. Segovia, eds. *They Were All Together in One Place?: Toward Minority Biblical Criticism*. Atlanta, GA: Society of Biblical Literature, 2009.

Balka, Christie, and Andy Rose, eds. *Twice Blessed: On Being Lesbian or Gay and Jewish*. Boston, MA: Beacon Press, 1989.

Bantum, Brian. *Redeeming Mulatto: A Theology of Race and Christian Hybridity*. Waco, TX: Baylor University Press, 2010.

Batchelor, Edward. *Homosexuality and Ethics*. New York: Pilgrim Press, 1980.

Bauer-Levesque, Angela. "Jeremiah." In Guest et al., *Queer Bible Commentary*, 386–93.

_____. Response to "Same-Sex Marriage and Relational Justice." *Journal of Feminist Studies in Religion* 20, no. 2 (Fall 2004): 112–17.

Beattie, Tina. "Queen of Heaven." In Loughlin, *Queer Theology*, 293–304.

Beckford, Robert. "Does Jesus Have a Penis?: Black Male Sexual Representation and Christology." *Theology and Sexuality*, no. 5 (Sept. 1996): 10–21.

Bernauer, James, and Jeremy Carrette, eds. *Michel Foucault and Theology: The Politics of Religious Experience*. Aldershot, UK: Ashgate, 2004.

Boer, Roland. "Yahweh as Top: A Lost Targum." In Stone, *Queer Commentary and the Hebrew Bible*, 75–105.

Bohache, Thomas. *Christology from the Margins*. London: SCM Press, 2008.

_____. "Pentecost Queered." In Guest et al., *Queer Bible Commentary*, 566–81.

Boisvert, Donald L. *Out on Holy Ground: Mediations on Gay Men's Spirituality*. Cleveland, OH: Pilgrim Press, 2000.

_____. *Sanctity and Male Desire: A Gay Reading of Saints*. Cleveland, OH: Pilgrim Press, 2004.

_____. "Talking Dirty About the Saints: Storytelling and the Politics of Desire." *Theology and Sexuality* 12, no. 2 (Jan. 2006): 165–80.

Boisvert, Donald L., and Robert E. Goss, eds. *Gay Catholic Priests and Clerical Sexual Misconduct: Breaking the Silence*. Binghamton, NY: Harrington Park Press, 2005.

Boswell, John. *Christianity, Social Tolerance, and Homosexuality: Gay People in Western Europe from the Beginning of the Christian Era to the Fourteenth Century*. Chicago: University of Chicago Press, 1980.

_____. *Same-Sex Unions in Premodern Europe*. New York: Vintage Books, 1994.

Bouldrey, Brian, ed. *Wrestling with the Angel: Faith and Religion in the Lives of Gay Men*. New York: Riverhead Books, 1995.

Boyd, Malcolm. *Gay Priest: An Inner Journey*. New York: St. Martin's Press, 1986.

Brant, Wil Rombotis. "Why Go to Church When You Can Drink with Mary?: Gaymale Clubculture as Religion Without Religion Against Ethics." *Theology and Sexuality*, no. 15 (Sept. 2001): 32–44.

Bray, Alan. *The Friend*. Chicago: University of Chicago Press, 2003.

_____. "Friendship, the Family and Liturgy: A Rite for Blessing Friendship in Traditional Christianity." *Theology and Sexuality*, no. 13 (Sept. 2000): 15–33.

Brintnall, Kent L. *Ecce Homo: The Male-Body-in-Pain as Redemptive Figure*. Chicago: University of Chicago Press, 2011 (forthcoming).

Brock, Rita Nakashima, and Susan Brooks Thistlethwaite. *Casting Stones: Prostitution and Liberation in Asia and the United States*. Minneapolis, MN: Fortress Press, 1996.

Brooten, Bernadette, J. *Love Between Women: Early Christian Responses to Female Homoeroticism*. Chicago: University of Chicago Press, 1996.

Brown, Judith C. *Immodest Acts: The Life of a Lesbian Nun in Renaissance Italy*. New York: Oxford University Press, 1988.

Brown, Terry, ed. *Other Voices, Other Worlds: The Global Church Speaks Out on Homosexuality*. New York: Church Publishing, 2006.

Browne, Kath, Sally R. Munt, and Andrew K.T. Yip. *Queer Spiritual Spaces: Sexuality and Sacred Places*. Farnham, UK: Ashgate, 2010.

Buchanan, Ian. *Oxford Dictionary of Critical Theory*. Oxford, UK: Oxford University Press, 2010.

Burrus, Virginia. "Queer Father: Gregory of Nyssa and the Subversion of Identity." In Loughlin, *Queer Theology*, 147–62.

_____. *The Sex Lives of Saints: An Erotics of Ancient Hagiography*. Philadelphia: University of Pennsylvania Press, 2004.

Burrus, Virginia, Mark D. Jordan, and Karmen MacKendrick. *Seducing Augustine: Bodies, Desires, Confessions*. New York: Fordham University Press, 2010.

Burrus, Virginia, and Catherine Keller. *Toward a Theology of Eros: Transfiguring Passion at the Limits of Discipline*. New York: Fordham University Press, 2006.

Busto, Rudy V. "The Gospel according to the Model Minority? Hazarding an Interpretation of Asian American Evangelical College Students." In Yoo, *New Spiritual Homes*, 169–87.

Cannon, Justin R. *Sanctified: An Anthology of Poetry by LGBT Christians*. Scotts Valley, CA: Createspace, 2008.

Carr, David M. *The Erotic Word: Sexuality, Spirituality, and the Bible*. Oxford, UK: Oxford University Press, 2003.

Carrette, Jeremy R. *Foucault and Religion: Spiritual Corporality and Political Spirituality*. London: Routledge, 2000.

Carrette, Jeremy, and Mary Keller. "Religions, Orientation and Critical Theory: Race, Gender and Sexuality at the 1998 Lambeth Conference." *Theology and Sexuality* 11 (Sept. 1999): 21–43.

Chellew-Hodge, Candace. *Bulletproof Faith: A Spiritual Survival Guide for Gay and Lesbian Christians*. San Francisco: Josey-Bass, 2008.

Cheng, Patrick S. "Faith, Hope and Love: Ending LGBT Teen Suicide," *Huffington Post* (Oct. 6, 2010), http://www.huffingtonpost.com/rev-patrick-s-cheng-phd/faith-hope-and-love-endin_b_749160.html.

_____. "Galatians." In Guest et al., *Queer Bible Commentary*, 624–29.

_____. "Hybridity and the Decolonization of Asian American and Queer Theologies." *Postcolonial Theology Network* (October 17, 2009). http://www.facebook.com/topic.php?uid=23694574926&topic=11026.

_____. "Multiplicity and Judges 19: Constructing a Queer Asian Pacific American Biblical Hermeneutic." *Semeia* 90/91 (2002): 119–33.

_____. "Reclaiming Our Traditions, Rituals, and Spaces: Spirituality and the Queer Asian Pacific American Experience." *Spiritus* 6 no. 2 (Fall 2006): 234–40.

_____. Response to "Same-Sex Marriage and Relational Justice." *Journal of Feminist Studies in Religion* 20, no. 2 (Fall 2004): 103–7.

_____. "Rethinking Sin and Grace for LGBT People Today." In Ellison and Douglas, *Sexuality and the Sacred*, 105–18.

_____. Review of *Queering Christ: Beyond Jesus Acted Up,* by Robert E. Goss. *Union Seminary Quarterly Review* 57, nos. 1–2 (2003): 158–60.

_____. "A Three-Part Sinfonia: Queer Asian Reflections on the Trinity." In Fernandez, *New Overtures* (forthcoming).

Cherry, Kittredge. *Art That Dares: Gay Jesus, Woman Christ, and More*. Berkeley, CA: Androgyne Press, 2007.

_____. *Jesus in Love*. Berkeley, CA: AndroGyne Press, 2006.

Cherry, Kittredge, and Zalmon Sherwood, eds. *Equal Rites: Lesbian and Gay Worship, Ceremonies, and Celebrations*. Louisville, KY: Westminster John Knox Press, 1995.

Clark, J. Michael. *Beyond Our Ghettos: Gay Theology in Ecological Perspective*. Cleveland, OH: Pilgrim Press, 1993.

_____. *A Defiant Celebration*. Garland, TX: Tangelwüld Press, 1990.

_____. *Defying the Darkness: Gay Theology in the Shadows*. Cleveland, OH: Pilgrim Press, 1997.

_____. *Diary of a Southern Queen: An HIV+ Vision Quest*. Dallas, TX: Monument Press, 1990.

_____. *Doing the Work of Love: Men and Commitment in Same-Sex Couples*. Harriman, TN: Men's Studies Press, 1999.

_____. *Gay Being, Divine Presence: Essays in Gay Spirituality (The Ganymede Papers)*. Las Colinas, TX: Tangelwüld Press, 1987.

_____. *A Lavender Cosmic Pilgrim: Further Ruminations on Gay Spirituality, Theology, and Sexuality*. Las Colinas, TX: Liberal Press, 1990.

_____. *A Place to Start: Toward an Unapologetic Gay Liberation Theology*. Dallas, TX: Monument Press, 1989.

Clark, J. Michael, and Michael L. Stemmeler, eds. *Spirituality and Community: Diversity in Lesbian and Gay Experience*. Las Colinas, TX: Monument Press, 1994.

Cleaver, Richard. *Know My Name: A Gay Liberation Theology*. Louisville, KY: Westminster John Knox Press, 1995.

Coakley, Sarah. "The Eschatological Body: Gender, Transformation, and God." *Modern Theology* 16, no. 1 (Jan. 2000): 61–73.

_____. "Living into the Mystery of the Holy Trinity: Trinity, Prayer, and Sexuality." In Rogers, *The Holy Spirit*, 44–52.

Comstock, Gary David. *Gay Theology Without Apology*. Cleveland, OH: Pilgrim Press, 1993.

_____. "One of the Family?: Gay Scholars and the Politics of the Academy." *Theology and Sexuality*, no. 1 (Sept. 1994): 89–95.

_____. *Unrepentant, Self-Affirming, Practicing: Lesbian/Bisexual/Gay People Within Organized Religion*. New York: Continuum, 1996.

_____. *A Whosoever Church: Welcoming Lesbians and Gay Men into African American Congregations*. Louisville, KY: Westminster John Knox Press, 2001.

_____. *The Work of a Gay College Chaplain: Becoming Ourselves in the Company of Others*. Binghamton, NY: Harrington Park Press, 2001.

Comstock, Gary David, and Susan E. Henking, eds. *Que(e)rying Religion: A Critical Anthology*. New York: Continuum, 1997.

Cone, James H. *Black Theology and Black Power*. New York: Harper and Row, 1969.

_____. *A Black Theology of Liberation*. New York: J.B. Lippincott, 1970.

_____. *God of the Oppressed*. New York: Seabury Press, 1975.

Cone, James H., and Gayraud S. Wilmore, eds. *Black Theology: A Documentary History, Volume II, 1980–1992*. Maryknoll, NY: Orbis Books, 1993.

Conner, Randy P., David Hatfield Sparks, and Mariya Sparks. *Cassell's Encyclopedia of Queer Myth, Symbol and Spirit: Gay, Lesbian, Bisexual, and Transgender Lore*. London: Cassell, 1997.

Córdova Quero, Hugo. "Risky Affairs: Marcella Althaus-Reid Indecently Queering Juan Luis Segundo's Hermeneutical Circle Propositions." In Isherwood and Jordan, *Dancing Theology in Fetish Boots*, 207–18.

Córdova Quero, Martín Hugo. "Friendship with Benefits: A Queer Reading of Aelred of Rievaulx and His Theology of Friendship." In Althaus-Reid and Isherwood, *The Sexual Theologian*, 26–46.

_____. "The Prostitutes Also Go into the Kingdom of God: A Queer Reading of Mary of Magdala." In Althaus-Reid, *Liberation Theology and Sexuality*, 81–110.

_____. "This Body Trans/Forming Me: Indecencies in Transgender/Intersex Bodies, Body Fascism and the Doctrine of the Incarnation." In Althaus-Reid and Isherwood, *Controversies in Body Theology*, 80–128.

Cornwall, Susannah. "Apophasis and Ambiguity: The 'Unknowingness' of Transgender." In Althaus-Reid and Isherwood, *Trans/formations*, 13–40.

_____. *Controversies in Queer Theology*. London: SCM Press, 2011 (forthcoming).

_____. "The *Kenosis* of Unambiguous Sex in the Body of Christ: Intersex, Theology and Existing 'for the Other.'" *Theology and Sexuality* 14, no. 2 (2008): 181–99.

_____. "'State of Mind' versus 'Concrete Set of Facts': The Contrasting of Transgender and Intersex in Church Documents on Sexuality." *Theology and Sexuality* 15, no. 1 (Jan. 2009): 7–28.

_____. "Stranger in Our Midst: The Becoming of the Queer God in the Theology of Marcella Althaus-Reid." In Isherwood and Jordan, *Dancing Theology in Fetish Boots*, 95–112.

Coulton, Nicholas, ed. *The Bible, the Church, and Homosexuality*. London: Darton, Longman and Todd, 2005.

Countryman, L. William. *Dirt, Greed and Sex: Sexual Ethics in the New Testament and Their Implications for Today*. Philadelphia, PA: Fortress Press, 1988.

Countryman, L. William, and M.R. Ritley. *Gifted by Otherness: Gay and Lesbian Christians in the Church*. Harrisburg, PA: Morehouse Publishing, 2001.

Crawley, Ashon T. "Circum-Religious Performance: Queer(ed) Black Bodies and the Black Church." *Theology and Sexuality* 14, no. 2 (Jan. 2008): 201–22.

Crowley, Paul G. *Unwanted Wisdom: Suffering, the Cross, and Hope*. New York: Continuum, 2005.

Daly, Mary. *Beyond God the Father: Toward a Philosophy of Women's Liberation*. Boston: Beacon Press, 1973.

Davies, Jon, and Gerard Loughlin. *Sex These Days: Essays on Theology, Sexuality and Society*. Sheffield, UK: Sheffield Academic Press, 1997.

D'Costa, Gavin. "Queer Trinity." In Loughlin, *Queer Theology*, 269–80.

de la Huerta, Christian. *Coming Out Spiritually: The Next Step*. New York: Jeremy T. Tarcher/Putnam, 1999.

De La Torre, Miguel A. "Confessions of a Latin Macho: From Gay Basher to Gay Ally." In De La Torre, *Out of the Shadows*, 59–75.

_____, ed. *Handbook of U.S. Theologies of Liberation*. St. Louis, MO: Chalice Press, 2004.

_____, ed. *Out of the Shadows, Into the Light: Christianity and Homosexuality*. St. Louis, MO: Chalice Press, 2009.

DiNovo, Cheri. *Qu(e)erying Evangelism: Growing a Community From the Outside In*. Cleveland, OH: Pilgrim Press, 2005.

Dormor, Duncan, and Jeremy Morris, eds. *An Acceptable Sacrifice?: Homosexuality and the Church*. London: SPCK, 2007.

Douglas, Ian T. "The Exigency of Times and Occasions: Power and Identity in the Anglican Communion Today." In Douglas and Kwok, *Beyond Colonial Anglicanism*, 25–46.

Douglas, Ian T., and Kwok Pui-lan, eds. *Beyond Colonial Anglicanism: The Anglican Communion in the Twenty-First Century*. New York: Church Publishing, 2001.

Douglas, Kelly Brown. *Sexuality and the Black Church: A Womanist Perspective*. Maryknoll, NY: Orbis Books, 1999.

Dowell, Susan. "Challenging Monogamy." *Theology and Sexuality*, no. 2 (March 1995): 84–103.

Drinkwater, Gregg, Joshua Lesser, and David Shneer. *Torah Queeries: Weekly Commentaries on the Hebrew Bible*. New York: New York University Press, 2009.

Duncan, Geoffrey. *Courage to Love: Liturgies for the Lesbian, Gay, Bisexual, and Transgender Community*. Cleveland, OH: Pilgrim Press, 2002.

Duraisingh, Christopher. "From Church-Shaped Mission to Mission-Shaped Church." *Anglican Theological Review* 92, no. 2 (Winter 2010): 7–28.

Dykstra, Laurel. "Jesus, Bread, Wine and Roses: A Bisexual Feminist at the Catholic Worker." In Kolodny, *Blessed Bi Spirit*, 78–88.

Dzmura, Noach, ed. *Balancing on the Mechitza: Transgender in Jewish Community*. Berkeley, CA: North Atlantic Books, 2010.

Easton, Dossie, and Janet W. Hardy. *Radical Ecstasy: SM Journeys to Transcendence*. Oakland, CA: Greenery Press, 2004.

Edgar, Andrew, and Peter Sedgwick. *Cultural Theory: The Key Concepts*. 2nd ed. London: Routledge, 2008.

Edwards, George R. *Gay/Lesbian Liberation: A Biblical Perspective*. New York: Pilgrim Press, 1984.

Ellison, Marvin M. *Erotic Justice: A Liberating Ethic of Sexuality*. Louisville, KY: Westminster John Knox Press, 1996.

—————. Response to "Same-Sex Marriage and Relational Justice." *Journal of Feminist Studies in Religion* 20, no. 2 (Fall 2004): 93–100.

—————. *Same-Sex Marriage?: A Christian Ethical Analysis*. Cleveland, OH: Pilgrim Press, 2004.

Ellison, Marvin M., and Kelly Brown Douglas, eds. *Sexuality and the Sacred: Sources for Theological Reflection*. 2nd ed. Louisville, KY: Westminster John Knox Press, 2010.

Ellison, Marvin M., and Sylvia Thorson-Smith, eds. *Body and Soul: Rethinking Sexuality as Justice-Love*. Cleveland, OH: Pilgrim Press, 2003.

Empereur, James L. *Spiritual Direction and the Gay Person*. New York: Continuum, 1998.

Eng, David L., and Alice Y. Hom. *Q&A: Queer in Asian America*. Philadelphia: Temple University Press, 1998.

Erzen, Tanya. *Straight to Jesus: Sexual and Christian Conversions in the Ex-Gay Movement*. Berkeley, CA: University of California Press, 2006.

Evans, Amie M., and Trebor Healey, eds. *Queer and Catholic*. New York: Routledge, 2008.

Farajajé-Jones, Elias. "Breaking Silence: Toward an In-the-Life Theology." In Cone and Wilmore, *Black Theology*, 139–59.

Fernandez, Eleazar, ed. *New Overtures*. Louisville, KY: Sopher Press, 2011 (forthcoming).

Fetner, Tina. *How the Religious Right Shaped Lesbian and Gay Activism*. Minneapolis: University of Minnesota Press, 2008.

Floyd-Thomas, Stacey M., and Anthony B. Pinn, eds. *Liberation Theologies in the United States: An Introduction*. New York: New York University Press, 2010.

Fortunato, John E. *AIDS, the Spiritual Dilemma*. San Francisco: Harper and Row, 1987.

Foucault, Michel. *Religion and Culture*. Selected and edited by Jeremy R. Carrette. New York: Routledge, 1999.

Foulke, Mary L., and Renee L. Hill. "We Are *Not* Your Hope for the Future: Being an Interracial Lesbian Family Living in the Present." In Goss and Strongheart, *Our Families, Our Values*, 243–49.

Fung, Richard. "Looking for My Penis: The Eroticized Asian in Gay Video Porn." In Eng and Hom, *Q&A*, 115–34.

Gabriele, Edward F. *Cloud Days and Fire Nights: Canticles for a Pilgrimage Out of Exile*. Winona, MN: Saint Mary's Press, 1997.

Garrigan, Siobhan. "Queer Worship." *Theology and Sexuality* 15, no. 2 (May 2009): 211–30.

Gearhart, Sally. "The Miracle of Lesbianism." In Gearhart and Johnson, *Loving Women / Loving Men*, 119–52.

Gearhart, Sally, and William R. Johnson, eds. *Loving Women / Loving Men: Gay Liberation and the Church*. San Francisco: Glide Publications, 1974.

Gebhardt, Daniel. *I Am This One Walking Beside Me: Meditations of a Gay HIV Positive Man*. Cleveland, OH: Pilgrim Press, 2005.

Gittings, Barbara B. "The Homosexual and the Church." In Weltge, *The Same Sex*, 146–55.

Glaser, Chris. *As My Own Soul: The Blessing of Same-Gender Marriage*. New York: Seabury Books, 2009.

_____. *Come Home!: Reclaiming Spirituality and Community as Gay Men and Lesbians*. San Francisco: Harper and Row, 1990.

_____. *Coming Out as Sacrament*. Louisville, KY: Westminster John Knox Press, 1998.

_____. *Coming Out to God: Prayers for Lesbians and Gay Men, Their Families and Friends*. Louisville, KY: Westminster John Knox Press, 1991.

_____. *Reformation of the Heart: Seasonal Meditations by a Gay Christian*. Louisville, KY: Westminster John Knox Press, 2001.

_____. *Uncommon Calling: A Gay Christian's Struggle to Serve the Church*. Louisville, KY: Westminster John Knox Press, 1988.

_____. *The Word Is Out: Daily Reflections on the Bible for Lesbians and Gay Men*. Louisville, KY: Westminster John Knox Press, 1994.

Godfrey, Donal. *Gays and Grays: The Story of the Gay Community at Most Holy Redeemer Catholic Church*. Lanham, MD: Lexington Books, 2007.

Gomes, Peter J. *The Good Book: Reading the Bible with Mind and Heart*. San Francisco: HarperSanFrancisco, 1996.

Good, D.J. "Reading Strategies for Biblical Passages on Same-Sex Relations." *Theology and Sexuality*, no. 7 (Sept. 1997): 70–82.

Good, Deirdre. *Jesus' Family Values*. New York: Church Publishing, 2006.

Gorrell, Paul J. "Rite to Party: Circuit Parties and Religious Experience." In Thumma and Gray, *Gay Religion*, 313–26.

_____. "The Roman Catholic Pedophilia Crisis and the Call to Erotic Conversion." *Theology and Sexuality* 12, no. 3 (May 2006): 251–62.

Goss, Robert E. *Jesus Acted Up: A Gay and Lesbian Manifesto*. San Francisco: HarperSanFrancisco, 1993.

_____. "Passionate Love for Christ: Out of the Closet, Into the Streets." In Kay, Nagle, and Gould, *Male Lust*, 297–304.

_____. "Proleptic Sexual Love: God's Promiscuity Reflected in Christian Polyamory." *Theology and Sexuality* 11, no. 1 (Sept. 2004): 52–63.

_____. *Queering Christ: Beyond Jesus Acted Up*. Cleveland, OH: Pilgrim Press, 2002.

Goss, Robert E., and Amy Adams Squire Strongheart, eds. *Our Families, Our Values: Snapshots of Queer Kinship*. Binghamton, NY: Harrington Park Press, 1997.

Goss, Robert E., and Mona West, eds. *Take Back the Word: A Queer Reading of the Bible*. Cleveland, OH: Pilgrim Press, 2000.

Graham, Larry Kent. *Discovering Images of God: Narratives of Care Among Lesbians and Gay Men*. Louisville, KY: Westminster John Knox Press, 1997.

Gramick, Jeannine, and Pat Furley. *The Vatican and Homosexuality: Reactions to the "Letter to the Bishops of the Catholic Church on the Pastoral Care of Homosexual Persons."* New York: Crossroad, 1988.

Gramick, Jeannine, and Robert Nugent, eds. *Voices of Hope: A Collection of Positive Catholic Writing on Gay and Lesbian Issues*. New York: Center for Homophobia Education, 1995.

Greenberg, Steven. *Wrestling with God and Men: Homosexuality in the Jewish Tradition*. Madison: University of Wisconsin Press, 2004.

Griffin, Horace L. *Their Own Receive Them Not: African American Lesbians and Gays in Black Churches*. Cleveland, OH: Pilgrim Press, 2006.

Gross, Sally. "Intersexuality and Scripture." *Theology and Sexuality* 11 (Sept. 1999): 65–74.

Guest, Deryn. *When Deborah Met Jael: Lesbian Biblical Hermeneutics*. London: SCM Press, 2005.

Guest, Deryn, Robert E. Goss, Mona West, and Thomas Bohache, eds. *The Queer Bible Commentary*. London: SCM Press, 2006.

Gutiérrez, Gustavo. *A Theology of Liberation: History, Politics, Salvation*. Maryknoll, NY: Orbis Books, 1973.

Haldeman, Scott. "A Queer Fidelity: Reinventing Christian Marriage." *Theology and Sexuality* 13, no. 2 (Jan. 2007): 137–52.

_____. "Receptivity and Revelation: A Spirituality of Gay Male Sex." In Krondorfer, *Men and Masculinities in Christianity and Judaism*, 381–92.

Hall, Donald E. *Queer Theories*. Basingstoke, UK: Palgrave Macmillan, 2003.

Haller, Tobias Stanislas. *Reasonable and Holy: Engaging Same-Sexuality*. New York: Seabury Books, 2009.

Halperin, David M. *Saint Foucault: Towards a Gay Hagiography.* New York: Oxford University Press, 1995.

Han, Arar, and John Hsu, eds. *Asian American X: An Intersection of 21st Century Asian American Voices.* Ann Arbor: University of Michigan Press, 2004.

Hanks, Tom. *The Subversive Gospel: A New Testament Commentary of Liberation.* Cleveland, OH: Pilgrim Press, 2000.

Hardy, Richard P. *Loving Men: Gay Partners, Spirituality, and AIDS.* New York: Continuum, 1998.

Harvey, Jennifer, Karin A. Case, and Robin Hawley Gorsline. *Disrupting White Supremacy from Within: White People on What We Need to Do.* Cleveland, OH: Pilgrim Press, 2004.

Hazel, Dann. *Witness: Gay and Lesbian Clergy Report from the Front.* Louisville, KY: Westminster John Knox Press, 2000.

Helminiak, Daniel A. *Sex and the Sacred: Gay Identity and Spiritual Growth.* Binghamton, NY: Harrington Park Press, 2006.

——————. *What the Bible Really Says About Homosexuality.* Millennium edition. Tajique, NM: Alamo Square Press, 2000.

Herman, Joanne. *Transgender Explained for Those Who Are Not.* Bloomington, IN: AuthorHouse, 2009.

Heyward, Carter. *Touching Our Strength: The Erotic as Power and the Love of God.* San Francisco: HarperSanFrancisco, 1989.

——————. "We're Here, We're Queer: Teaching Sex in Seminary." In Ellison and Thorson-Smith, *Body and Soul*, 78–96.

Hibbert, Giles. "Gay Liberation in Relation to Christian Liberation." In Macourt, *Towards a Theology of Gay Liberation*, 91–99.

Hill, Renee L. "Who Are We for Each Other?: Sexism, Sexuality and Womanist Theology." In Cone and Wilmore, *Black Theology*, 345–51.

Hill, Renée Leslie. "Disrupted/Disruptive Movements: Black Theology and Black Power 1969 / 1999." In Hopkins, *Black Faith and Public Talk*, 138–49.

Hinnant, Olive Elaine. *God Comes Out: A Queer Homiletic.* Cleveland, OH: Pilgrim Press, 2007.

Hipsher, B.K. "God Is a Many Gendered Thing: An Apophatic Journey to Pastoral Diversity." In Althaus-Reid and Isherwood, *Trans/formations*, 92–104.

Hollywood, Amy. "Sexual Desire, Divine Desire; Or, Queering the Beguines." In Burrus and Keller, *Towards a Theology of Eros*, 119–33.

Hopkins, Dwight N., ed. *Black Faith and Public Talk: Critical Essays on James H. Cone's Black Theology and Black Power.* Maryknoll, NY: Orbis Books, 1999.

Howells, Edward, and Peter Tyler. *Sources of Transformation: Revitalising Christian Spirituality.* London: Continuum, 2010.

Hunt, Mary E. *Fierce Tenderness: A Feminist Theology of Friendship.* New York: Crossroad, 1991.

——————. "Same-Sex Marriage and Relational Justice." *Journal of Feminist Studies in Religion* 20, no. 2 (Fall 2004): 83–92.

Hunt, Mary E., and Diann L. Neu, eds. *New Feminist Christianity: Many Voices, Many Views.* Woodstock, VT: SkyLight Paths Publishing, 2010.

Hunt, Stephen, ed. *Contemporary Christianity and LGBT Sexualities.* Farnham, UK: Ashgate, 2009.

Isherwood, Lisa. *The Power of Erotic Celibacy: Queering Heteropatriarchy.* London: T&T Clark, 2006.

Isherwood, Lisa, and Mark D. Jordan, eds. *Dancing Theology in Fetish Boots: Essays in Honour of Marcella Althaus-Reid.* London: SCM Press, 2010.

Jagose, Annamarie. *Queer Theory: An Introduction.* New York: New York University Press, 1996.

Jakobsen, Janet R., and Ann Pellegrini. *Love the Sin: Sexual Regulation and the Limits of Religious Tolerance.* New York: New York University Press, 2003.

James, G. Winston, and Lisa C. Moore, eds. *Spirited: Affirming the Soul and Black Gay/Lesbian Identity.* Washington, DC: Redbone Press, 2006.

Jantzen, Grace M. "Off the Straight and Narrow: Toward a Lesbian Theology." *Theology and Sexuality*, no. 3 (Sept. 1995): 58–76.

Jarrett, Emmett. *To Heal the Sin-Sick Soul: Toward a Spirituality of Anti-Racist Ministry.* New London, CT: Episcopal Urban Caucus, 1996.

Jennings, Theodore W. *Jacob's Wound: Homoerotic Narrative in the Literature of Ancient Israel.* New York: Continuum, 2005.

——————. *The Man Jesus Loved: Homoerotic Narratives from the New Testament.* Cleveland, OH: Pilgrim Press, 2003.

——————. "YHWH as Erastes." In Stone, *Queer Commentary and the Hebrew Bible*, 36–74.

Johnson, Bill. "The Good News of Gay Liberation." In Gearhart and Johnson, *Loving Women/Loving Men*, 91–117.

Johnson, Jay Emerson. *Dancing with God: Anglican Christianity and the Practice of Hope*. Harrisburg, PA: Morehouse Publishing, 2005.

———. "Searching for Religious Eroticism: The Solitary and the Ocular in Gay Religious Studies." *Theology and Sexuality*, no. 16 (March 2002): 45–53.

Johnson, Toby. *Gay Perspective: Things Our Homosexuality Tells Us About the Nature of God and the Universe*. Los Angeles: Alyson Books, 2003.

———. *Gay Spirituality: The Role of Gay Identity in the Transformation of Human Consciousness*. Maple Shade, NJ: Lethe Press, 2004.

Jones, H. Kimball. *Toward a Christian Understanding of the Homosexual*. New York: Association Press, 1966.

Jones, Serene. *Trauma and Grace: Theology in a Ruptured World*. Louisville, KY: Westminster John Knox Press, 2009.

Jordan, Mark D., ed. *Authorizing Marriage?: Canon, Tradition, and Critique in the Blessing of Same-Sex Unions*. Princeton, NJ: Princeton University Press, 2006.

———. "'Baptizing' Queer Characters." In Kamitsuka, *Embrace of Eros*, 151–63.

———. *Blessing Same-Sex Unions: The Perils of Queer Romance and the Confusions of Christian Marriage*. Chicago: University of Chicago Press, 2005.

———. *The Ethics of Sex*. Oxford, UK: Blackwell Publishers, 2002.

———. "God's Body." In Loughlin, *Queer Theology*, 281–92.

———. *The Invention of Sodomy in Christian Theology*. Chicago: University of Chicago Press, 1997.

———. *The Silence of Sodom: Homosexuality in Modern Catholicism*. Chicago: University of Chicago Press, 2000.

———. "Sodomites and Churchmen: The Theological Invention of Homosexuality." In Bernauer and Carrette, *Michel Foucault and Theology*, 233–44.

———. *Telling Truths in Church: Scandal, Flesh, and Christian Speech*. Boston: Beacon Press, 2003.

Kamitsuka, Margaret D., ed. *The Embrace of Eros: Bodies, Desires, and Sexuality in Christianity*. Minneapolis, MN: Fortress Press, 2010.

Kay, Kerwin, Jill Nagle, and Baruch Gould, eds. *Male Lust: Pleasure, Power, and Transformation*. Binghamton, NY: Harrington Park Press, 2000.

Kelly, Michael Bernard. "A Potential for Transformation: Gay Men and the Future of Christian Spirituality." In Howell and Tyler, *Sources of Transformation*, 183–94.

———. *Seduced by Grace: Contemporary Spirituality, Gay Experience, and Christian Faith*. Melbourne, Australia: Clouds of Magellan, 2007.

Kim, Michael. "Out and About: Coming of Age in a Straight White World." In Han and Hsu, *Asian American X*, 139–48 (written under a pseudonym).

Knauss, Stefanie. "Transcendental Relationships?: A Theological Reflection on Cybersex and Cyber-Relationships." *Theology and Sexuality* 15, no. 3 (Sept. 2009): 329–48.

Koch, Timothy R. "A Homoerotic Approach to Scripture." *Theology and Sexuality*, no. 14 (Jan. 2001): 10–22.

Kolakowski, Victoria S. "Toward a Christian Ethical Response to Transsexual Persons." *Theology and Sexuality*, no. 6 (March 1997): 10–31.

Kolodny, Debra R., ed. *Blessed Bi Spirit: Bisexual People of Faith*. New York: Continuum, 2000.

Kondrath, William M. *God's Tapestry: Understanding and Celebrating Differences*. Herndon, VA: Alban Institute, 2008.

Kornegay, EL. "Queering Black Homophobia: Black Theology as a Sexual Discourse of Transformation." *Theology and Sexuality* 11, no. 1 (Sept. 2004): 29–51.

Krondorfer, Björn. *Men and Masculinities in Christianity and Judaism: A Critical Reader*. London: SCM Press, 2009.

———. "Who's Afraid of Gay Theology? Men's Studies, Gay Scholars, and Heterosexual Silence." In Krondorfer, *Men and Masculinities in Christianity and Judaism*, 421–36.

Kuefler, Mathew, ed. *The Boswell Thesis: Essays on Christianity, Social Tolerance, and Homosexuality*. Chicago: University of Chicago Press, 2006.

Kujawa-Holbrook, Sheryl A., and Fredrica Harris Thompsett. *Born of Water, Born of Spirit: Supporting the Ministry of the Baptized in Small Congregations*. Herndon, VA: Alban Institute, 2010.

Kumashiro, Kevin K., ed. *Restoried Selves: Autobiographies of Queer Asian/Pacific American Activists*. Binghamton, NY: Harrington Park Press, 2004.

Kundtz, David J., and Bernard S. Schlager. *Ministry Among God's Queer Folk: LGBT Pastoral Care*. Cleveland, OH: Pilgrim Press, 2007.

Kwok Pui-lan. "Asian and Asian American Churches." In Siker, *Homosexuality and Religion*, 59–62.

_____. "Body and Pleasure in Postcoloniality." In Isherwood and Jordan, *Dancing Theology in Fetish Boots*, 31–43.

_____. *Postcolonial Imagination and Feminist Theology*. Louisville, KY: Westminster John Knox Press, 2005.

_____. "Touching the Taboo: On the Sexuality of Jesus." In Ellison and Douglas, *Sexuality and the Sacred*, 119–34.

Kwok Pui-lan, Don H. Compier, and Joerg Rieger, eds. *Empire and the Christian Tradition: New Readings of Classical Theologians*. Minneapolis, MN: Fortress Press, 2007.

Lake, Catherine, ed. *Recreations: Religion and Spirituality in the Lives of Queer People*. Toronto: Queer Press, 1999.

Lakeland, Paul. "Ecclesiology, Desire, and the Erotic." In Kamitsuka, *The Embrace of Eros*, 247–59.

Law, Eric H.F. "A Spirituality of Creative Marginality." In Comstock and Henking, *Que(e)rying Religion*, 343–46.

Lea, Jeffrey. *For Another Flock: Daily Advent and Christmas Meditations for Gay and Lesbian Christians*. Cleveland, OH: Pilgrim Press, 2005.

Lee, Jeanette Mei Gim. "Queerly a Good Friday." In Kumashiro, *Restoried Selves*, 81–86.

Levine, Amy-Jill, ed. *A Feminist Companion to John*. Vol. 1. Cleveland, OH: Pilgrim Press, 2003.

Lewin, Ellen. *Recognizing Ourselves: Ceremonies of Lesbian and Gay Commitment*. New York: Columbia University Press, 1998.

Liew, Tat-siong Benny. "Queering Closets and Perverting Desires: Cross-Examining John's Engendering and Transgendering Word Across Different Worlds." In Bailey et al., *They Were All Together in One Place?*, 251–88.

_____. "(Co)Responding: A Letter to the Editor." In Stone, *Queer Commentary and the Hebrew Bible*, 182–92.

Lim, Leng Leroy. "'The Bible Tells Me to Hate Myself': The Crisis in Asian American Spiritual Leadership." *Semeia* 90/91 (2002): 315–22.

_____. "Exploring Embodiment." In Ragsdale, *Boundary Wars*, 58–77.

_____. "Webs of Betrayal, Webs of Blessings." In Eng and Hom, *Q & A*, 323–34.

Lim, Leng, Kim-Hao Yap, and Tuck-Leong Lee. "The Mythic-Literalists in the Province of South Asia." In Brown, *Other Voices, Other Worlds*, 58–76.

Lindsey, William D. "The AIDS Crisis and the Church: A Time to Heal." *Theology and Sexuality*, no. 2 (March 1995): 11–37.

Linzey, Andrew, and Richard Kirker. *Gays and the Future of Anglicanism: Responses to the Windsor Report*. Winchester, UK: O Books, 2005.

Long, Ron. "A Place for Porn in a Gay Spiritual Economy." *Theology and Sexuality*, no. 11 (March 2002): 21–31.

Long, Ronald E. "Heavenly Sex: The Moral Authority of an Impossible Dream." *Theology and Sexuality* 11, no. 3 (May 2005): 31–46.

Long, Ronald E., and J. Michael Clark. *AIDS, God, and Faith*. Las Colinas, TX: Monument Press, 1992.

Lopata, Mary Ellen. *Fortunate Families: Catholic Families with Lesbian Daughters and Gay Sons*. Victoria, Canada: Trafford Publishing, 2003.

Lorde, Audre. "Uses of the Erotic: The Erotic as Power." In Ellison and Douglas, *Sexuality and the Sacred*, 73–77.

Loughlin, Gerard. "God's Sex." In Milbank, Pickstock, and Ward, *Radical Orthodoxy*, 143–62.

_____. "Introduction: The End of Sex." In Loughlin, *Queer Theology*, 1–34.

_____. "Omphalos." In Loughlin, *Queer Theology*, 115–27.

_____, ed. *Queer Theology: Rethinking the Western Body*. Malden, MA: Blackwell, 2007.

Love, Cindi. *Would Jesus Discriminate?: The 21st Century Question*. Victoria, Canada: Trafford Publishing, 2008.

Love, Joshua L., and Metropolitan Community Church Global HIV/AIDS Ministry. *Uncommon Hope: A DVD Enhanced Curriculum Reflecting the Heart of the Church for People Affected by HIV/AIDS*. Victoria, Canada: Trafford Publishing, 2009.

Lytle, Julie. "Virtual Incarnations: Exploration of Internet-Mediated Interaction as Manifestations of the Divine." *Religious Education* 105, no. 4 (July 2010): 395–412.

Macey, David. *Dictionary of Critical Theory*. London: Penguin Books, 2000.

Machacek, David W., and Melissa M. Wilcox, eds. *Sexuality and the World's Religions*. Santa Barbara, CA: ABC-CLIO, 2003.

Macourt, Malcolm, ed. *Towards a Theology of Gay Liberation*. London: SCM Press, 1977.

Maher, Michael. *Being Gay and Lesbian in a Catholic High School: Beyond the Uniform*. Binghamton, NY: Harrington Park Press, 2001.

Marshall, Joretta L. *Counseling Lesbian Partners*. Louisville, KY: Westminster John Knox Press, 1997.

Martin, Dale B. *Sex and the Single Savior: Gender and Sexuality in Biblical Interpretation*. Louisville, KY: Westminster John Knox Press, 2006.

Martin, Del, and Phyllis Lyon. "A Lesbian Approach to Theology." In Oberholtzer, *Is Gay Good?*, 213–20.

Martin, Joan M. *More Than Chains and Toil: A Christian Work Ethic of Enslaved Women*. Louisville, KY: Westminster John Knox Press, 2000.

Matzko, David McCarthy. "The Relationship of Bodies: A Nupital Hermeneutics of Same-Sex Unions." *Theology and Sexuality*, no. 8 (March 1998): 96–112.

McCleary. Rollan. *A Special Illumination: Authority, Inspiration and Heresy in Gay Spirituality*. London: Equinox Publishing, 2004.

McGinley, Dugan. *Acts of Faith, Acts of Love: Gay Catholic Autobiographies as Sacred Texts*. New York: Continuum, 2004.

McLaughlin, Eleanor. "Feminist Christologies: Re-Dressing the Tradition." In Stevens, *Reconstructing the Christ Symbol*, 118–49.

McNeill, John J. *Both Feet Firmly Planted in Midair: My Spiritual Journey*. Louisville, KY: Westminster John Knox Press, 1998.

_____. *The Church and the Homosexual*. 4th ed. Boston: Beacon Press, 1993.

_____. *Freedom, Glorious Freedom: The Spiritual Journey to the Fullness of Life for Gays, Lesbians, and Everyone Else*. Boston: Beacon Press, 1995.

_____. *Sex as God Intended: A Reflection on Human Sexuality as Play*. Maple Shade, NJ: Lethe Press, 2008.

_____. *Taking a Chance on God: Liberating Theology for Gays, Lesbians, and Their Lovers, Families, and Friends*. Boston: Beacon Press, 1996.

Metropolitan Community Church of New York. *The Gay Christian* 1, no. 5 (September 2002).

Metropolitan Community Churches, *TRANSFormative Church Ministry Program* (October 4, 2010).

Michaelson, Jay. "Chaos, Law, and God: The Religious Meanings of Homosexuality." *Michigan Journal of Gender and Law* 15, no. 1 (2008): 41–119.

_____. *God in Your Body: Kabbalah, Mindfulness and Embodied Spiritual Practice*. Woodstock, VT: Jewish Lights Publishing, 2007.

_____. *God vs. Gay?: The Religious Case for Equality*. Boston: Beacon Press, 2011 (forthcoming).

Milbank, John, Catherine Pickstock, and Graham Ward, eds. *Radical Orthodoxy: A New Theology*. London: Routledge, 1999.

Miner, Jeff, and John Tyler Connoley. *The Children Are Free: Reexamining the Biblical Evidence on Same-Sex Relationships*. Indianapolis, IN: Jesus Metropolitan Community Church, 2002.

Mollenkott, Virginia Ramey. *Omnigender: A Trans-Religious Approach*. Cleveland, OH: Pilgrim Press, 2001.

_____. *Sensuous Spirituality: Out from Fundamentalism*. New York: Crossroad, 1992.

_____. "Trans-forming Feminist Christianity." In Hunt and Neu, *New Feminist Christianity*, 127–37.

Mollenkott, Virginia Ramey, and Vanessa Sheridan. *Transgender Journeys*. Cleveland, OH: Pilgrim Press, 2003.

Irene Monroe. "Between a Rock and a Hard Place: Struggling with the Black Church's Heterosexism and the White Queer Community's Racism." In De La Torre, *Out of the Shadows*, 39–58.

_____. "When and Where I Enter, Then the Whole Race Enters with Me: Que(e)rying Exodus." In Goss and West, *Take Back the Word*, 82–91.

Montefiore, H.W. "Jesus, The Revelation of God." In Pittenger, *Christ for Us Today*, 101–16

Moon, Dawne. *God, Sex, and Politics: Homosexuality and Everyday Theologies*. Chicago: University of Chicago Press, 2004.

Moore, Darnell L. "Theorizing the 'Black Body' as a Site of Trauma: Implications for Theologies of Embodiment." *Theology and Sexuality* 15, no. 2 (May 2009), 175–88.

Moore, Gareth. *A Question of Truth: Christianity and Homosexuality*. London: Continuum, 2003.

Moore, Stephen D. *God's Beauty Parlor and Other Queer Spaces In and Around the Bible*. Stanford, CA: Stanford University Press, 2001.

_____. *God's Gym: Divine Male Bodies of the Bible*. New York: Routledge, 1996.

Morrison, Melanie. *The Grace of Coming Home: Spirituality, Sexuality, and the Struggle for Justice*. Cleveland, OH: Pilgrim Press, 1995.

Morse, Christopher. "Has Ms. Spaulding Been Addressed?" *Anglican Theological Review* 90, no. 3 (Summer 2008): 549–55.

Murray, Paul. *Life in Paradox: The Story of a Gay Catholic Priest*. Winchester, UK: O Books, 2008.

Myers, David G., and Letha Dawson Scanzoni. *What God Has Joined Together?: A Christian Case for Gay Marriage*. San Francisco: HarperSanFrancisco, 2005.

Nausner, Michael. "Toward Community Beyond Gender Binaries: Gregory of Nyssa's Transgendering as Part of His Transformative Eschatology." *Theology and Sexuality*, no. 16 (2002): 55–65.

Nelson, James B. *Embodiment: An Approach to Sexuality and Christian Theology*. Minneapolis, MN: Augsburg Publishing House, 1978.

Nelson, James B., and Sandra P. Longfellow. *Sexuality and the Sacred: Sources for Theological Reflection*. Louisville, KY: Westminster John Knox Press, 1994.

Nimmons, David. *The Soul Beneath the Skin: The Unseen Hearts and Habits of Gay Men*. New York: St. Martin's Griffin, 2002.

Nissinen, Martti. *Homoeroticism in the Biblical World: A Historical Perspective*. Minneapolis, MN: Fortress Press, 1998.

Norris, Richard A. "Homosexuality, Ethics, and the Church: An Essay by the Late Richard Norris with Responses." *Anglican Theological Review* 90, no. 3 (Summer 2008): 419–623.

Nugent, Robert, ed. *A Challenge to Love: Gay and Lesbian Catholics in the Church*. New York: Crossroad, 1984.

Nugent, Robert, and Jeannine Gramick. *Building Bridges: Gay and Lesbian Reality and the Catholic Church*. Mystic, CT: Twenty-Third Publications, 1992.

Oberholtzer, W. Dwight, ed. *Is Gay Good?: Ethics, Theology, and Homosexuality*. Philadelphia: Westminster Press, 1971.

Oliver, Juan M.C. "Why Gay Marriage?" *Journal of Men's Studies* 4, no. 3 (1996): 209–24.

O'Neill, Craig, and Kathleen Ritter. *Coming Out Within: Stages of Spiritual Awakening for Lesbians and Gay Men*. San Francisco: HarperSanFrancisco, 1992.

O'Riordan, Kate, and Heather White. "Virtual Believers: Queer Spiritual Practice Online." In Browne, Munt, and Yip, *Queer Spiritual Spaces*, 199–230.

Oxford University Press. *Oxford English Dictionary Online*, at http://www.oed.com.

Percy, Martyn, ed. *Intimate Affairs: Sexuality and Spirituality in Perspective*. London: Darton, Longman and Todd, 1997.

Perry, Troy. *Don't Be Afraid Anymore: The Story of Reverend Troy Perry and the Metropolitan Community Churches*. New York: St. Martin's Press, 1990.

_____. *The Lord Is My Shepherd And He Knows I'm Gay*. Los Angeles: Nash Publishing, 1972.

Peterson, Thomas V. "Gay Men's Spiritual Experience in the Leather Community." In Thumma and Gray, *Gay Religion*, 337–50.

Petrella, Ivan. "Queer Eye for the Straight Guy: The Making Over of Liberation Theology, A Queer Discursive Approach." In Althaus-Reid, *Liberation Theology and Sexuality*, 33–49.

Piazza, Michael S. *Gay by God: How to Be Lesbian or Gay and Christian*. Dallas, TX: Sources of Hope Publishing, 2008.

Pinn, Anthony B. *Embodiment and the New Shape of Black Theological Thought*. New York: New York University Press, 2010.

Pittenger, Norman, ed. *Christ for Us Today*. London: SCM Press Ltd., 1968.

_____. *Time for Consent: A Christian's Approach to Homosexuality*. London: SCM Press, 1976.

Pomfret, Scott. *Since My Last Confession: A Gay Catholic Memoir*. New York: Arcade Publishing, 2008.

Pronk, Pim. *Against Nature?: Types of Moral Argumentation Regarding Homosexuality*. Grand Rapids, MI: William B. Eerdmans Publishing, 1993.

Ragsdale, Katherine Hancock, ed. *Boundary Wars: Intimacy and Distance in Healing Relationships*. Cleveland, OH: Pilgrim Press, 1996.

Rinella, Jack. *Philosophy in the Dungeon: The Magic of Sex and Spirit.* Chicago: Rinella Editorial Services, 2006.

Rodman, Edward. "A Lost Opportunity?: An Open Letter to the Leadership of the Episcopal Church." In Jarrett, *To Heal the Sin-Sick Soul,* 65–80.

Rogers, Eugene F. *The Holy Spirit: Classic and Contemporary Readings.* Malden, MA: Wiley-Blackwell, 2009.

_____. *Sexuality and the Christian Body: Their Way into the Triune God.* Oxford, UK: Blackwell Publishers, 1999.

_____. "The Shape of the Body and the Shape of Grace." In Rogers, *Sexuality and the Christian Body,* 237–49.

Rogers, Jack. *Jesus, the Bible, and Homosexuality: Explode the Myths, Heal the Church.* Louisville, KY: Westminster John Knox Press, 2006.

Roscoe, Will. *Queer Spirits: A Gay Men's Myth Book.* Boston: Beacon Press, 1995.

Rudy, Kathy. *Sex and the Church: Gender Homosexuality, and the Transformation of Christian Ethics.* Boston: Beacon Press, 1997.

_____. "'Where Two or More Are Gathered': Using Gay Communities as a Model for Christian Sexual Ethics." *Theology and Sexuality,* no. 4 (March 1996): 81–99.

S., Vanessa. *Cross Purposes: On Being Christian and Crossgendered.* Decatur, GA: Sullivan Press, 1996.

Savastano, Peter. "Gay Men as Virtuosi of the Holy Art of Bricolage and as Tricksters of the Sacred." *Theology and Sexuality* 14, no. 1 (Sept. 2007): 9–28.

Say, Elizabeth A., and Mark R. Kowalewski. *Gays, Lesbians, and Family Values.* Cleveland, OH: Pilgrim Press, 1998.

Scanzoni, Letha Dawson, and Virginia Ramey Mollenkott. *Is the Homosexual My Neighbor?: A Positive Christian Response.* Rev. and updated ed. San Francisco: HarperSanFrancisco, 1994.

Schippert, Claudia. "Too Much Trouble?: Negotiating Feminist and Queer Approaches in Religion." *Theology and Sexuality* 11 (Sept. 1999): 44–63.

Schneider, Laurel C. *Beyond Monotheism: A Theology of Multiplicity.* London: Routledge, 2008.

_____. "Homosexuality, Queer Theory, and Christian Theology." In Krondorfer, *Men and Masculinities in Christianity and Judaism,* 63–76.

_____. "What Race Is Your Sex?" In Harvey, Case, and Gorsline, *Disrupting White Supremacy from Within,* 142–62.

Scroggs, Robin. *The New Testament and Homosexuality.* Philadelphia, PA: Fortress Press, 1983.

Shaw, M. Thomas. *Conversations with Scripture and with Each Other: Spiritual Formation for Lay Leaders.* Lanham, MD: Rowman and Littlefield, 2008.

Sheffield, Tricia. "Performing Jesus: A Queer Counternarrative of Embodied Transgression." *Theology and Sexuality* 14, no. 3 (May 2008): 233–58.

Sheridan, Vanessa. *Crossing Over: Liberating the Transgendered Christian.* Cleveland, OH: Pilgrim Press, 2001.

Shinnick, Maurice. *This Remarkable Gift: Being Gay and Catholic.* St. Leonards, Australia: Allen and Unwin, 1997.

Shore-Goss, Robert E. "Gay and Lesbian Theologies." In Floyd-Thomas and Pinn, *Liberation Theologies in the United States,* 181–208.

Siker, Jeffrey S., ed. *Homosexuality and Religion: An Encyclopedia.* Westport, CT: Greenwood Press, 2007.

_____. "Queer Theology." In Siker, *Homosexuality and Religion,* 188–90.

Smith, Morton. *The Secret Gospel: The Discovery and Interpretation of the Secret Gospel According to Mark.* New York: Harper and Row, 1973.

Sneed, Roger A. *Representations of Homosexuality: Black Liberation Theology and Cultural Criticism.* New York: Palgrave Macmillan, 2010.

Spencer, Daniel T. *Gay and Gaia: Ethics, Ecology, and the Erotic.* Cleveland, OH: Pilgrim Press, 1996.

_____. "Lesbian and Gay Theologies." In De La Torre, *Handbook of U.S. Theologies of Liberation,* 264–73.

Steinberg, Leo. *The Sexuality of Christ in Renaissance Art and in Modern Oblivion.* 2nd ed. Chicago: University of Chicago Press, 1996.

Stemmeler, Michael L., and J. Michael Clark, eds. *Constructing Gay Theology.* Las Colinas, TX: Monument Press, 1990.

_____, eds. *Gay Affirmative Ethics.* Las Colinas, TX: Monument Press, 1993.

_____, eds. *Homophobia and the Judeo-Christian Tradition.* Dallas, TX: Monument Press, 1990.

Stemmeler, Michael L., and José Ignacio Cabezón, eds. *Religion, Homosexuality, and Literature*. Las Colinas, TX: Monument Press, 1992.

Stevens, Maryanne, ed. *Reconstructing the Christ Symbol: Essays in Feminist Christology*. New York: Paulist Press, 1993.

Stone, Ken. "'Do Not Be Conformed to This World': Queer Reading and the Task of the Preacher." *Theology and Sexuality* 13, no. 2 (Jan. 2007): 153–66.

_____. *Practicing Safer Texts: Food, Sex and Bible in Queer Perspective*. London: T&T Clark International, 2005.

_____, ed. *Queer Commentary and the Hebrew Bible*. Cleveland, OH: Pilgrim Press, 2001.

_____. "Queering the Canaanite." In Althaus-Reid and Isherwood, *The Sexual Theologian*, 110–34.

_____. "Safer Text: Reading Biblical Laments in the Age of AIDS." *Theology and Sexuality*, no. 10 (March 1999): 16–27.

Storey, William G. *A Book of Prayer for Gay and Lesbian Christians*. New York: Crossroad Publishing, 2002.

Stryker, Susan. *Transgender History*. Berkeley, CA: Seal Press, 2008.

Stuart, Elizabeth. *Gay and Lesbian Theologies: Repetitions with Critical Difference*. Aldershot, UK: Ashgate, 2003.

_____. *Just Good Friends: Towards a Lesbian and Gay Theology of Relationships*. London: Mowbray, 1995.

_____. "Making No Sense: Liturgy as Queer Space." In Isherwood and Jordan, *Dancing Theology in Fetish Boots*, 113–23.

_____. "The Priest at the Altar: The Eucharistic Erasure of Sex." In Althaus-Reid and Isherwood, *Trans/formations*, 127–38.

_____. "Queering Death." In Althaus-Reid and Isherwood, *The Sexual Theologian*, 58–70.

_____. "Sacramental Flesh." In Loughlin, *Queer Theology*, 65–75.

_____. "Sex in Heaven: The Queering of Theological Discourse on Sexuality." In Davies and Loughlin, *Sex These Days*, 184–204.

_____. "Sexuality: The View from the Font." *Theology and Sexuality*, no. 11 (Sept. 1999): 9–20.

_____. *Spitting at Dragons: Towards a Feminist Theology of Sainthood*. New York: Mowbray, 1996.

Stuart, Elizabeth, Andy Braunston, Malcolm Edwards, John McMahon, and Tim Morrison. *Religion Is a Queer Thing: A Guide to the Christian Faith for Lesbian, Gay, Bisexual and Transgendered People*. Cleveland, OH: Pilgrim Press, 1997.

Suárez, Margarita. "Reflections on Being Latina and Lesbian." In Comstock and Henking, *Que(e)rying Religion*, 347–50.

Sullivan, Nikki. *A Critical Introduction to Queer Theory*. New York: New York University Press, 2003.

Sweasey, Peter. *From Queer to Eternity: Spirituality in the Lives of Lesbian, Gay and Bisexual People*. London: Cassell, 1997.

Swidler, Arlene, ed. *Homosexuality and World Religions*. Valley Forge, PA: Trinity Press International, 1993.

Switzer, David K. *Pastoral Care of Gays, Lesbians, and Their Families*. Minneapolis, MN: Fortress Press, 1999.

Tanis, Justin. *Trans-Gendered: Theology, Ministry, and Communities of Faith*. Cleveland, OH: Pilgrim Press, 2003.

Thumma, Scott, and Edward R. Gray, eds. *Gay Religion*. Walnut Creek, CA: AltaMira Press, 2005.

Tigert, Leanne McCall. *Coming Out Through Fire: Surviving the Trauma of Homophobia*. Cleveland, OH: United Church Press, 1999.

_____. *Coming Out While Staying In: Struggles and Celebrations of Lesbians, Gays, and Bisexuals in the Church*. Cleveland, OH: United Church Press, 1996.

Tigert, Leanne McCall, and Maren C. Tirabassi, eds. *Transgendering Faith: Identity, Sexuality, and Spirituality*. Cleveland, OH: Pilgrim Press, 2004.

Tigert, Leanne McCall, and Timothy Brown, eds. *Coming Out Young and Faithful*. Cleveland, OH: Pilgrim Press, 2001.

Tonstad, Linn Marie. "Sexual Difference and Trinitarian Death: Cross, Kenosis, and Hierarchy in the Theo-Drama." *Modern Theology* 26, no. 4 (Oct. 2010): 603–31.

Townes, Emilie M. "Marcella Althaus-Reid's *Indecent Theology*: A Response." In Isherwood and Jordan, *Dancing Theology in Fetish Boots*, 61–67.

_____. Response to "Same-Sex Marriage and Relational Justice." *Journal of Feminist Studies in Religion* 20, no. 2 (Fall 2004): 100–103.

Trible, Phyllis. *Texts of Terror: Literary-Feminist Readings of Biblical Narratives*. Philadelphia, PA: Fortress Press, 1984.

Troeger, Thomas H. "No More Scapegoats." In Hinnant, *God Comes Out*, 40–47.

Truluck, Rembert. *Steps to Recovery from Bible Abuse*. Gaithersburg, MD: Chi Rho Press, 2000.

Turner, William B. *A Genealogy of Queer Theory*. Philadelphia: Temple University Press, 2000.

Vasey, Michael. *Strangers and Friends: A New Exploration of Homosexuality and the Bible*. London: Hodder and Stoughton, 1995.

Ward, Graham. "The Displaced Body of Jesus Christ." In Milbank, Pickstock, and Ward, *Radical Orthodoxy*, 163–81.

_____. "There Is No Sexual Difference." In Loughlin, *Queer Theology*, 76–85.

Watkins, Durrell. *Wrestling with God Without Getting Pinned: Old Stories, New Thoughts, and Progressive Spirituality*. Denver, CO: Outskirts Press, 2010.

Weakland, Rembert G. *A Pilgrim in a Pilgrim Church: Memoirs of a Catholic Archbishop*. Grand Rapids, MI: William B. Eerdmans Publishing, 2009.

Weiss, David R. *To the Tune of a Welcoming God: Lyrical Reflections on Sexuality, Spirituality, and the Wideness of God's Welcome*. Minneapolis, MN: Langdon Street Press, 2008.

Wells, Howard R. "Gay God, Gay Theology." *The Gay Christian: Journal of the New York Metropolitan Community Church* 1, no. 5 (September 1972): 6–8.

Weltge, Ralph W., ed. *The Same Sex: An Appraisal of Homosexuality*. Philadelphia: Pilgrim Press, 1969.

West, Mona. "The Raising of Lazarus: A Lesbian Coming Out Story." In Levine, *Feminist Companion to John*, 143–58.

_____. "Reading the Bible as Queer Americans: Social Location and the Hebrew Scriptures." *Theology and Sexuality*, no. 10 (March 1999): 28–42.

White, Heather Rachelle. "Proclaiming Liberation: The Historical Roots of LGBT Religious Organizing, 1946–1976." *Nova Religio* 11, no. 4 (2008): 102–19.

White, Mel. *Stranger at the Gate: To Be Gay and Christian in America*. New York: Plume/Penguin Books, 1995.

Wilchins, Riki. *Queer Theory, Gender Theory: An Instant Primer*. Los Angeles: Alyson Books, 2004.

Wilcox, Melissa M. *Coming Out in Christianity: Religion, Identity, and Community*. Bloomington: Indiana University Press, 2003.

_____. "Innovation in Exile: Religion and Spirituality in Lesbian, Gay, Bisexual, and Transgender Communities." In Machacek and Wilcox, *Sexuality and the World's Religions*, 323–57.

Williams, Robert. *Just as I Am: A Practical Guide to Being Out, Proud, and Christian*. New York: HarperPerennial, 1992.

Wills, Lawrence M. *Not God's People: Insiders and Outsiders in the Biblical World*. Lanham, MD: Rowman and Littlefield, 2008.

Wilson, Nancy. *Our Tribe: Queer Folks, God, Jesus, and the Bible*. San Francisco, HarperSanFrancisco, 1995.

Wolkomir, Michelle. *Be Not Deceived: The Sacred and Sexual Struggles of Gay and Ex-Gay Christian Men*. New Brunswick, NJ: Rutgers University Press, 2006.

Wood, Robert W. *Christ and the Homosexual (Some Observations)*. New York: Vantage Press, 1960.

Yee, Gale A. *Poor Banished Children of Eve: Women as Evil in the Hebrew Bible*. Minneapolis, MN: Fortress Press, 2003.

Yip, Andrew K.T. "Gay Male Christians' Perceptions of the Christian Community in Relation to Their Sexuality." *Theology and Sexuality*, no. 8 (March 1998): 40–51.

Yoo, David K., ed. *New Spiritual Homes: Religion and Asian Americans*. Honolulu: University of Hawai'i Press, 1999.

Index

About the Author

Patrick S. Cheng is the Assistant Professor of Historical and Systematic Theology at Episcopal Divinity School in Cambridge, Massachusetts. He holds a Ph.D., M.Phil., and M.A. from Union Theological Seminary in New York, a J.D. from Harvard Law School, and a B.A. from Yale College. Patrick is a contributor to the religion section of the *Huffington Post* and is an ordained minister with the Metropolitan Community Churches. His writings have appeared in a number of publications, including the second edition of *Sexuality and the Sacred (WJK)* and *The Queer Bible Commentary* (SCM). For more information about Patrick, see his website at http://www.patrickcheng.net.